# Growing Catholics
A Journey from *Cradle* to *Catholic*

ॐ

*Denise Sullivan Barnes*

iUniverse, Inc.
New York  Bloomington

Growing Catholics
A Journey from Cradle to Catholic

Copyright © 2010 Denise Sullivan Barnes

All rights reserved. No part of this book may be used or reproduced by any means, graphic, electronic, or mechanical, including photocopying, recording, taping or by any information storage retrieval system without the written permission of the publisher except in the case of brief quotations embodied in critical articles and reviews.

iUniverse books may be ordered through booksellers or by contacting:

iUniverse
1663 Liberty Drive
Bloomington, IN 47403
www.iuniverse.com
1-800-Authors (1-800-288-4677)

Because of the dynamic nature of the Internet, any Web addresses or links contained in this book may have changed since publication and may no longer be valid. The views expressed in this work are solely those of the author and do not necessarily reflect the views of the publisher, and the publisher hereby disclaims any responsibility for them.

ISBN: 978-1-4502-3091-9 (pbk)
ISBN: 978-1-4502-3093-3 (cloth)
ISBN: 978-1-4502-3092-6 (ebk)

Printed in the United States of America

iUniverse rev. date: 5/24/2010

*All that I have written
seems to me like so much straw compared to
what I have seen and what has been revealed to me.*

*St. Thomas Aquinas*

# Contents

Preface ......................................................................... ix
Introduction .................................................................. xi

## Part I  Assess ............................................................ 1

1. Cradle Catholic ........................................................ 3
2. The Three Little Pigs Revisited ................................. 6
3. It Is Easier to See with Your Eyes Open .................. 8
4. Who's the Boss? ..................................................... 12
5. Because I Said So ................................................... 16

## Part II  Commit ......................................................... 21

6. Are You a Chicken or a Pig? ................................... 23
7. What Chocolate Taught Me ................................... 27
8. Stepping Up to the Plate ........................................ 31
9. Homeschooling ...................................................... 35

## Part III  Pray ............................................................. 41

10. In God We Trust ................................................... 43
11. Broccoli, Shrimp, and the Rosary .......................... 47
12. Will You Be My Friend? ....................................... 50
13. The Eleventh Step ................................................ 52
14. Father, Son, and Holy Syrup ................................. 56

## Part IV  Celebrate — 59

- 15. Can I Get a Witness? — 61
- 16. Let Me Entertain You — 64
- 17. May the Force Be with You — 68
- 18. Catholic Calisthenics — 72
- 19. Casual Sundays — 75
- 20. Love Is Like a Rose — 78

## Part V  Learn — 83

- 21. An "F" in Religion — 85
- 22. Explain It to Me Like I'm a Four-Year-Old — 88
- 23. The "God Loves Us" Rule — 91
- 24. Carrots or Potato Chips? — 95
- 25. I'm Not Qualified — 98
- 26. Why Do Catholics Do That? — 102

## Part VI  Surround and Share — 105

- 27. How to Sell Your Home to a Catholic in Ninety Days — 107
- 28. Sticks and Stones May Break My Bones — 109
- 29. Frank or Frances? — 113
- 30. American Idol — 117
- 31. The Little Red Hen — 120

## Part VII  Grow — 125

- 32. Raising the Bar — 127
- 33. Rembrandt Did It — 130
- 34. Fall into the Fall Leaves — 132
- 35. A Triple Dog Dare — 134

# Preface

I have always wanted to sing beautifully, but try as I may, I simply cannot sing on key—much to the chagrin of those within earshot. I used to envy those who had this gift. Then somewhere along my life's journey, I just decided to enjoy writing. Quite frankly, my mother encouraged me to read as a child, but I was too busy playing to make time for it. No one really encouraged me to write, and I don't really recall being taught how to write. So, as I sit to write this book, I can only thank God for giving me this gift, which comes from no one else. I have written a lot in my lifetime, and as I nourish what I now recognize as God's gift to me, I can only apologize for taking so long to give His gift back. I no longer envy the beautiful singers. I am thankful they share their gifts, and I hope you enjoy my gift as much as I enjoy listening to beautiful voices in song.

I dedicate this book to my husband, Mike, without whom you would not be reading any of these words. He is my biggest fan, my devoted companion on my ongoing faith journey, and the wind beneath my wings. Because I truly witness God's love through him, he has been my constant reminder of my call to share this piece of work with you.

I also attribute this book's completion in part to my mother, who never gave up on the book I was perpetually writing and provided the occasional nudge.

I thank my dad, who gave me the gift of faith, all those who have been a part of my journey in some way, and my children, who thought this was a cool idea and who have lived their lives alongside one relentless Catholic mother.

# Introduction

**I Did Not Shoot That Lady**

I was raised Catholic—*a cradle Catholic*—and am now the mother of three children and an employee of the Catholic Church. However, because of my experiences as a Catholic child, a Catholic parent, and a Catholic educator who catechizes youth and adults, I made the decision not to raise my children Catholic. As I shared this information with others, I came to realize the need to write this book explaining my decision.

I once learned a lesson in communication when I was asked to read the phrase, "I did not shoot that lady," repeating it with the emphasis on different words. For example, I could say, "*I* did not shoot that lady," or I could say, "I did not *shoot* that lady," or "I did not shoot *that* lady." Notice how the meaning of this sentence changes depending on where the emphasis is. So when I say, "I decided not to raise my children Catholic," what I mean is I decided not to *raise* Catholic children. Instead, I decided to *grow* Catholic children. It is my hope that as you read this book, the difference between *raising* Catholics and *growing* Catholics becomes clear and that you decide to *grow* Catholic children.

There are two stories bound in these pages highlighting my journey from cradle to Catholic. One is my story about being *raised* Catholic, including my life as a nonpracticing Catholic; the other is the story of my decision to *grow* as a Catholic and to *grow* Catholic children. Through the sharing of the first story, I came to know my story is not unique. I learned that many people have been raised Catholic and continue to raise other Catholics, all without growing. Perhaps you have a similar story. The more others shared with me, the more disheartened I became over the possibility of the perpetuation of experiences like mine for Catholic children today and in the future.

It became clear to me that many Catholic children do not know their faith, or perhaps don't even want to know their faith. I soon discovered the reason for this lack of knowledge may be that the parents of these children do not know their faith. I began to worry about the future of the Catholic Church and the generations of Catholics who may never know the joy that comes from having strong faith and a relationship with Christ.

I read a booklet called *National Study of Youth and Religion: Analysis of the Population of Catholic Teenagers and Their Parents*, produced in December 2004 and published by the National Federation for Catholic Youth Ministry, Washington DC. It exposed me to alarming statistics, which I will share throughout this book as "NFCYM data." The results of this study are published in a book entitled *Soul Searching: The Religious and Spiritual Lives of American Teenagers*. Scripture quotations come from the New American Bible and reference notations of (CCC) refer to the Catechism of the Catholic Church.

I come to you through these pages in my role as a relentless Catholic mother. I am not a perfect parent (as my children remind me from time to time), nor am I a perfect Catholic (as my need for reconciliation reminds me). I am not special for having the experiences I have had with my faith. I am still growing as a Catholic and have much to learn myself. My hope is that I can motivate you to learn from my missteps (the times I walked in the darkness of not knowing and growing) and my joys (the times I walked in the light of Christ).

In this book, I will share with you the steps I used in my conversion from nonpracticing Catholic to growing Catholic in the hopes that you can use these same steps to grow in your faith. In each chapter, I present my personal stories and the steps I took to grow as a Catholic. I challenge you to look at your faith and encourage you to take similar steps to help you on your faith journey, so that my newfound joy will be your joy also. I pray that this book opens your eyes as a Catholic parent to the real importance and significance of your role as the first and primary teacher of faith and that it will inspire you to *grow* Catholics in your life.

## How to Eat an Elephant

Please know that my new spiritual journey has been over twenty years in the making. As you read about my journey and discover all the time and energy I put into growing, it may seem overwhelming when you think about starting your own journey. Chances are you have been given a head start through your baptism and upbringing like me. However, I want to encourage you as you read this book to think about eating an elephant. When I am overwhelmed by the many chores and tasks I have to do, my husband always asks me, "Do you know how to eat an elephant?"

I respond with the same answer he has given me the past twelve years, "One bite at a time." It is his reminder to me to just start. Then I take the next step and the next until I realize I have tackled the entire job, one step at a time. When people want to make many changes in their lives, the best and most successful approach is to set short-term goals to change one thing at a time, as any good self-help book would encourage them to do. It is easy to predict some failure for someone who sets goals to simultaneously lose weight, switch careers, join a gym, give up chocolate, go back to school, quit smoking, and learn to speak a foreign language. In the same way, I would recommend you look at each of the sections of this book as your short-term goals for change toward the long-term goal of growing.

I encourage you to read this book with the same patience and nurturing that a gardener gives his or her creations. Just as a gardener might savor all the changes that come in each bud that sprouts while awaiting the final product, notice the changes in your faith life and celebrate the beautiful *fruit* that results.

This book is what I call a bathroom read, which means you can easily read a chapter in one "sitting." I am fully aware that the entire contents can be read in one day. I know this because I have made my husband do it a few times during the editing phase. If you are anything like me, you will want to plow through the entire book or at least skip to the back and see how it ends. If you feel the need to do this, promise yourself you will go back and reread it. Here's why. This book is about change. I once heard it takes forty days to change a habit, and I find it an interesting coincidence that the number forty often illustrates a time of trial and testing in scripture.[1] Perhaps this also has something to do with the fact that the season of Lent is forty days long.

---

1    To name a few:
"For forty days and forty nights heavy rain poured down on the earth" (Gen. 7:12).
"The Israelites ate this manna for forty years, until they came to settled land" (Exod. 16:35).
"Forty days more and Nineveh shall be destroyed" (Jon. 3:4).
"He remained in the desert for forty days, tempted by Satan" (Mark 1:13).
"He presented himself alive to them by many proofs after he had suffered, appearing to them during forty days and speaking about the kingdom of God" (Acts 1:3).

My suggestion is to read each section and then make yourself a specific plan for change based on the material in that section. Write your plan down as a to-do list, and share it with at least one other person. Place your written plan somewhere where you will see it every day. Once you have planned your work, work your plan. Only you know when you are ready to move on to the next section or the next goal for your spiritual growth, but perhaps forty days is a good place to start. During the forty days following the completion of a section, focus only on your goals pertaining to that section.

Refer back to only those sections from time to time until you feel ready to take on the next change in your spiritual growth. Think of your goals for each section as your short-term goals, and think of those of the final section, *Grow*, as your long-term ones. Once you have completed the book, go back from time to time and start over. To this day, I use this approach on my continuing journey. I would be disappointed if this book did not show signs of wear and tear with earmarked pages and a worn cover. I have learned in my life that faith is not something to set on a shelf and let collect dust. Each time I think, "I've got it," a new opportunity for growth comes along and slaps me in the face.

Finally, any success I have had growing in faith has happened only because I started in the first place. I hope this book becomes your starting point, and I also hope you will continue way beyond this book as I still do today—one bite at a time! I have asked the Holy Spirit to guide you as you read and to send you the courage to challenge yourself as a Catholic parent. With that said, welcome to the fruits of my labors—my "seeds" awaiting the fruitful garden where Catholics grow.

---

"The kingdom of heaven is like a mustard seed, which a man took and planted in his field. Though it is the smallest of all your seeds, yet when it grows, it is the largest of garden plants" (Matt. 13:31–32).

# Part I
# Assess

*Let's Begin by Reviewing
Your Faith Foundation*

# 1
# Cradle Catholic

My faith life started in the small town of Osceola, Iowa—the place where I was baptized. This is where I began being *raised* Catholic. I am called a "cradle Catholic," a term which refers to someone who has been Catholic since the cradle, not since birth. No one is *born* Catholic; it is a conscious and loving choice made by parents who wish to bequeath the awesome gift of faith. I thank my parents for giving me this gift. Knowing what I know today, I truly understand what a precious gift this is. Looking back, I know I did not appreciate it nearly enough.

As a child, there were many things my parents gave me that I did not appreciate. Immunization shots, for example, caused me pain. I would not voluntarily ask to be stuck with a long needle. As a parent myself now, however, I can appreciate the immunizations I received. Perhaps the author Mark Twain said it best when he said, "When I was a boy of fourteen, my father was so ignorant I could hardly stand to have the old man around. But when I got to be twenty-one, I was astonished at how much the old man had learned in seven years." In other words, it is good our parents make decisions for us as infants, because we are too young to make many decisions ourselves and to appreciate the value of such decisions. Parents give children immunization shots out of love. Similarly, parents have children baptized out of love. If you are not yet convinced of the great love and brilliance your parents demonstrated by having you baptized, just sit tight.

I attended a Catholic school in Shawnee, Kansas. I received the sacraments of reconciliation, Communion, and confirmation. Our family never skipped a Sunday Mass. We prayed before the evening meal, and my brother and sisters and I played pretend church at home with squished bread for our hosts and fruit punch for wine. At the time, I believed we were good Catholics, but looking back, I feel some things were missing. I don't recall discussing faith at home, reading the Bible as a family, or sharing prayer outside the traditional before-meal blessing.

When I graduated from a public high school near Columbia, Missouri, I was a Catholic adult. I headed to college and into the real world as a Catholic—a Catholic who had no real idea about what it meant to be Catholic or why I continued to go to Mass every Sunday. Through no fault of those who tried to help me grow spiritually, I was headed to college as a Catholic who was *taller* than the Catholic I was in elementary and high school, but I had the spiritual maturity of an eighth-grader.

In college, my faith was tested by those around me. I was questioned about Catholicism, and I had no answers to the questions I was asked. I could not explain why I was Catholic, why I honored Mary, how Christ was truly present in the Eucharist, why I had to tell my sins to a priest, why I couldn't recite scripture, why I believed in purgatory even though this word isn't in the Bible, why I prayed to saints, and where the Pope got his authority. I was exposed to many other ideas and practices of faith. I enjoyed a few philosophy courses and began to question the ideas imposed on me by my parents and teachers. Self-righteously, I decided to begin my own personal relationship with God and even wrote a very passionate paper on the bureaucracy of the Catholic Church in protest of Catholicism. It was clear that I had simply inherited my parents' faith and had no ownership of it myself.

In my second year of college, I found my idea of a personal relationship with Christ a dismal failure. I was not looking for Jesus in my life. I was no longer close to the Eucharist, and I had very little commitment to my faith. My faith weakened until I became a nonpracticing Catholic.

In retrospect, I know the problem was my faith foundation. I left for college with a foundation that was not strong. When faced with temptations, my faith was washed away. Over two thousand years ago, Jesus told my story.

Everyone who listens to these words of mine and acts on them will be like a wise man who built his house on rock. The rain fell, the floods came, and the winds blew and buffeted the house. But it did not collapse; it had been set solidly on rock. And everyone who listens to these words of mine but does not act on them will be like a fool who built his house on sand. The rain fell, the floods came, and the winds blew and buffeted the house. And it collapsed and was completely ruined. (Matt. 7:24–27)

Jesus's teaching here was just as relevant to me in 1983 as it was when Jesus spoke so long ago. My house (my faith) collapsed because of my weak foundation (my ignorance or laziness about hearing Jesus's words). Assess your foundation now. It will determine the type of faith foundation you build for your children. Is your foundation strong enough to fulfill your baptismal promise to bring them up in the practice of the faith? Does your faith collapse when challenged? Will their faith collapse when challenged, or will they have the tools needed to defend their faith and grow?

---

"According to the grace of God given to me, like a wise master builder I laid a foundation, and another is building upon it. But each one must be careful how he builds upon it, for no one can lay a foundation other than the one that is there, namely, Jesus Christ" (1 Cor. 3:10–11).

# 2
# The Three Little Pigs Revisited

I recently started a bedtime story with my youngest daughter and made a discovery that led to a fulfilling moment in my faith journey. I found my faith story in the classic tale of "The Three Little Pigs." As I read this story, I saw myself in college as the pig with the straw house, the straw house representing my faith. I did not take much care in building it. The Big Bad Wolf was Satan, temptations, darkness, sin, and those questioning my faith. Because my faith (the straw house) was weak, these temptations made it collapse (they huffed and puffed and blew my house down). The pig with the house of brick represented those who did not let temptation destroy their faith because they took care to nourish and grow it.

The foundations of the three little pigs' homes parallel the types of foundation we build for children regarding faith. The importance of a strong house or foundation seems clear in the story of "The Three Little Pigs." However, when it comes to the abstract idea of a foundation for faith, the importance does not seem so obvious. If parents were really trying to protect children from a "big, bad wolf," I have no doubt they would build the strongest house possible. However, because our eyes don't see the devil like we see a big, bad wolf, we don't worry about building strong houses of faith. We often forget the devil works in the exact same manner as the Big Bad Wolf. He tempts us toward sin and can prevent us from having eternal life with Christ. The devil tempted me in college and had some success, and he continues to tempt me today. The Bible tells us about the devil's temptation of Jesus during his forty days in the desert (Matt. 4:1–11). After reading this, I realized that if the devil would make an effort to tempt even Christ, there is no reason to believe anyone would be exempt from the devil's work. As you attempt to grow in faith, you must make yourself aware of those who are tempting you to turn away from Christ. Once you have identified them, you must remove them from your environment as much as possible or you must evangelize them by your example.

Chances are you have been tempted by the devil. Maybe you have been involved in spreading gossip. Perhaps you let someone convince you it was okay to skip Mass for a football game. You may have refused to forgive someone, or perhaps you have been persuaded to support the death penalty by a politician. Who is the devil using to tempt you in your life? In other words, who or what is the Big Bad Wolf that is huffing and puffing at your door? More important, who or what will the devil use to get to your child? Is the sin and death the devil offers something you want to protect your child from experiencing?

Recognize the value in building strong foundations of faith for children. The strongest foundations come from those who know God, love God, and serve God. If you have a desire for your children to have true happiness, you must help them build a house of faith that promotes these three ideals. Furthermore, with a proper foundation, your children will continue to grow in your absence. I implore you, as a Catholic child whose house was buffeted and collapsed, to make a commitment to this important step in their spiritual growth. Help your children build houses of brick, not straw, so they can keep the wolf of temptations out and experience the joy a life in Christ offers.

---

"Unless the Lord build the house, they labor in vain who build" (Ps. 127:1).

# 3
# It Is Easier to See with Your Eyes Open

You may wonder how I can read the story of the "Three Little Pigs" and find God. I bet I have read that story a thousand times in my life without noticing scripture in the pages. Perhaps you have, too. My discovery in this story came because I was more aware of God in my life at that moment. The more I become aware of God, the more I notice Him. The more I notice Him today, the more joy I experience. In other words, the path to growing in faith is paved for those who are open to receiving it. This is where my journey from a tall Catholic to a growing Catholic begins—with an open heart.

Having an open heart is as simple as looking for Christ in those you encounter every day. It's hearing the Word of God through prayer and scripture and opening your mind to grow in faith and Christ's love. Each of us has the ability to see with spiritual eyes. Even the blind can have their eyes opened spiritually. In the Gospel of John, there is a story of a man born blind. In the beginning of the story, we hear Jesus speaking:

> "While I am in the world, I am the light of the world." When he said this, he spat on the ground and made clay with the saliva, and smeared the clay on [the blind man's] eyes, and said to him,

"Go wash in the Pool of Siloam" (which means sent). So he went and washed, and came back able to see. (John 9:5–7)

Not only does Jesus cure this man's physical blindness, but he opens the man's heart (or spiritual eyes). When Jesus asked the blind man if he believed in the Son of Man, "He said, 'I do believe, Lord,' and he worshiped him" (John 9:35–38).

Seeing with spiritual eyes involves making Christ a part of each day and being aware of Him working in your life. It is seeing Christ's love in a kind gesture or a smile; it is seeing Him in the beauty of the nature that surrounds you, and it is seeing Christ's message in the story of the "Three Little Pigs." For example, I was giving my youngest daughter hugs and kisses for doing a kind deed. I explained she made Jesus very happy with her kind deed, and since we can't always see Jesus, sometimes he uses people like Mommy to give His hugs to people.

Today, I spend time with God, and I am continually looking for Jesus at work in my life. It has made all the difference. I know the value of my relationship with God, and it has allowed me to grow. The more I look, the more I find His love, His compassion, His joy, and His mercy in the faces of those with whom I share my life. For me, this transition from a person who was going through life without recognizing God's presence to one who acknowledges Him daily is nothing short of proof that the Holy Spirit exists and is looking for open hearts to fill.

If you are interested in growing Catholic children or growing in faith, begin by opening your heart to the possibilities of Christ, and I promise the Holy Spirit will fill that openness. Parents' eyes, ears, lips, minds, and hearts must be *open* in order to nurture growth in their children's faith life. It is also important to remember that no matter where you are in your own faith, there is always opportunity for growth. As Catholics, we are continually called to conversion and must be open to it.

If you think Jesus cannot be found in our world today, it is because you are not looking hard enough. I recognize Him in every smile given to me, in every act of kindness and love, and sometimes, I even recognize Him in a song.

When I was in high school, Bryan Adams was one of my favorite pop singers. In truth, the fact that I had a crush on the singer played a big role in my love of his songs. One of my favorite songs was one titled,

"Everything I Do (I Do It for You)." The song tells the story of someone who has such deep love for another that he would do anything for that person. In high school, I just enjoyed the beat and the thoughts of this handsome singer. When I met my husband many years later, this song became a song that reminded me of him. It became one of "our songs," because I truly felt it spoke of the kind of love my husband had for me. As an adult, the song took on a new meaning for me; no longer was my enjoyment of it about the handsome singer. One Sunday, I was driving home alone from a religious training course. The course did much to open my eyes to Christ in my world. When I turned on the radio, our Bryan Adams' song came on. I was amazed, however, to discover that the song in that moment was about Christ's love for me—not about a high-school crush or my husband. I listened to the words so differently that afternoon. Then a song by Rod Stewart called, "Have I Told You Lately That I Love You" was played, and it too became a song about my relationship with Christ. In my car that Sunday afternoon, I had come to the conclusion that *every* true love song could be a song about Christ's love. It was such a powerful moment of discovery for me on my journey to opening my eyes to see Christ that I can't help but find him everywhere today.

Once I got home from my drive, I called my husband and children into the living room to share my newfound discovery. I made them listen to the song they had heard all too many times one more time, but I asked them to listen with different ears. My children thought I was nuts, and my oldest daughter said, "Why do you think everything has to be about God?"

I replied, "Because everything is about God. If it's not about God, then what is life about?"

I had not yet convinced her in that moment, but as I was recounting the story to my children, we all learned something about seeing Christ in those around us. As I said out loud to them, "I realized the song was really about Christ," I immediately recognized why I was confused in thinking it was actually about my husband. It was because he is the place I see Christ the most.

So, I challenge you to listen to a few love songs; see Christ in every smile you receive. Look for the fruits of the Spirit: love, joy, peace, patience, kindness, goodness, faithfulness, gentleness, and self-control, and there you will *see* Christ. He is always there; you just need to open your eyes and notice Him. Make a commitment today to show Christ to others through your actions. Start by making a commitment to have an open heart as you read on through the pages of this book. Then, make a commitment to open your eyes to seeing Christ at work in your life every day.

---

"'For I was hungry and you gave me food, I was thirsty and you gave me drink, a stranger and you welcomed me, naked and you clothed me, ill and you cared for me, in prison and you visited me.'

"Then the righteous will answer him and say, 'Lord, when did we see you hungry and feed you, or thirsty and give you drink? …'

"And the king will say to them in reply, 'Amen, I say to you, whatever you did for one of these least brothers of mine, you did for me'" (Matt. 25:35–40).

# 4
# Who's the Boss?

Congratulations! You are the parent. As a child, you may have fantasized about being a parent. Perhaps you remember telling your own parents, "I can't wait until I have kids. I'm going to let them do whatever they want." Well, now is your chance. You've made it to the point in your life where you get to determine the rules.

Contrary to the belief of the two-year-old or adolescent who says, "You're not the boss of me," you are the boss! What kind of boss will you be? What rules will you truly make?

As a parent, chances are good you do not let your children do whatever they want as you may have once told your parents you would. There is a clear, scientific explanation for this. In a child contemplating parenting styles, the prefrontal lobe (the part of the brain that makes decisions) is not fully developed. As an adult with a fully developed brain, you understand the consequences of letting children do whatever they want. This understanding leads parents to the idea of setting boundaries (also known as "being mean").

There is a poem by Bobbie Pingaro called "The Meanest Mother" that begins with the complaints of a son whose mother made him eat healthy, take baths, get plenty of rest, do chores, tell the truth, be responsible, be respectful, and study. The poem concludes with the following line:

*Using this as a background, I am trying to raise my three children. I stand a little taller and I am filled with pride when my children call me mean.*
*Because, you see, I thank God, He gave me the meanest mother in the whole world.*

Children may believe parents exist for the sole purpose of being mean to them. However, parents exist to guide children until each child's prefrontal lobe is fully developed (in the early to mid twenties for most). It is this scientific fact regarding brain development that prevents parents from allowing a one-year-old to make the decision about whether or not to get an immunization shot that involves sticking a sharp needle in his or her arm, which will hurt. A one-year-old cannot discern the benefits of such a painful experience. This is why the job of parenting is so important. There is a true, scientific need for parental intercession and guidance.

Spiritually, the need for parental intercession is also evident. In a summary of the NFCYM data, Robert McCarty[2] reports, "The single most important influence on the religious and spiritual lives of adolescents is their parents." Although it is not a guarantee, the best predictor of faith in a child is the faith of his or her parents; that is, if a parent has strong faith, his or her children will have strong faith. The NFCYM data provides information about how often Catholic teenagers in the study attended Mass and how often they would attend Mass if it were up to them (rather than their parents). The exact same percentage (36 percent) was true for both questions, thus acknowledging the parental influence. Teenagers like their parents to believe they are not paying attention to them, but the research consistently tells us the opposite is true.

In the 1980s, there was a television sitcom called *Who's the Boss?* starring actor Tony Danza. Tony's character was a live-in housekeeper to a single mother and her child. In the show, it was sometimes unclear whether the housekeeper or the mother was in charge of the house. It was comical. What is not comical, however, is the fact we can probably recognize this same situation existing between parents and children in today's reality. Children like to persuade parents that they know what is

---

2   National Federation for Catholic Youth Ministry, Inc. (Washington DC, 2005), see Introduction for details.

best. Children seek empowerment. For years, parents have empowered children to choose what breakfast cereal to place in the grocery cart, but today, this empowerment does not always stop in the grocery store aisle. Some children are empowered by parents to decide issues their underdeveloped brains may not be ready to handle such as, "Do I need to go to church? Do I need to have faith?"

As the boss of my own children, I decided I could let them choose what cereal to buy, but I never let them determine whether or not we went to church on Sunday. In reminiscing on their early childhood, my first two children joke about how they each asked only one time in their lives, "Do we have to go to church?"

On each occasion, the inquisitive child was greeted with a horrified gasp and a nonnegotiable dissertation which could best be summarized by the following sample: "God gave you life, and He gave His only son who died on the cross for you and you don't even want to give Him one hour a week in return? Do you realize how lucky you are to have a mother who loves you so much that she wants you to share in this chance to be with Christ today at Mass? Did I mention Christ died for you?"

In conclusion, they were reminded who was the boss. I simply said, "When you are the parent, you get to make that decision for your children. Until then, I'm the boss and I get to decide. Now go get dressed." From the way the story is told by my children, the horrified gasp was enough to send the message. Either way, they knew they had a boss who was much more passionate about Mass than about cereal.

If you are counting, you may have noticed I have not given this dissertation to my third child. I can only assume the first two children had a secret conference with her to warn her of the hazards of such an inquiry because she has yet to ask the question, "Do we have to go to church?" Now that my first two children have left the nest, I continue to do my part by asking about Mass, reminding them of holy days, inviting them to church and other religious events, giving them religious materials to read, and advising them to pray. Furthermore, I pray for all of my children to appreciate the gift of faith, and I give thanks to God for each day they choose to have faith in their life. This prayer is a simple, but imperative, step I encourage all parents to take in helping their children grow in faith.

Now, stop and think about the decisions you empower your

children to make, and then think about your baptismal promise to bring your child up in the practice of the faith. Are you fulfilling your commitment while their prefrontal lobe is being developed? You are the boss. Do not let a child convince you they are more qualified than you to make important decisions about faith, because even science tells us otherwise.

Science aside, even Jesus experienced parents. Joseph and Mary guided Jesus and taught Him many things. Our all-powerful God certainly could have placed Jesus on earth without an earthly mother or father. He created Adam and Eve without parents. Through the birth of Jesus, our creator seems to be confirming the importance of parents. If not for the intercession of my parents, I may not know faith today. It is possible, through the work of the Holy Spirit, to come to know faith without parental influence, but my experience in teaching children and adults confirms that parents make a difference. So at least until children leave the proverbial nest, parental intercession is necessary. That is the job of parent, boss, mean person, and rule maker. Whether you are making a decision about going to Mass or which cereal to buy, please realize the importance of this ministry. Just as in the poem at the beginning of this chapter, I ask you as you read on: do you love your children enough to let them call you "mean" for doing what's right, even when it's not popular?

---

"Children obey your parents in the Lord, for this is right. Honor your father and mother. This is the first commandment with a promise, that it may go well with you and that you may have a long life on earth. Fathers, do not provoke your children to anger, but bring them up with the training and instruction of the Lord" (Eph. 6:1–4).

# 5
# Because I Said So

One of the unique privileges of being a parent is being able to say, "Because I said so" to children. We have probably all said these words or a similar version of them when our children asked questions like, "Why do I have to brush my teeth?" or "Why do I have to go to bed?"

The phrase, "Because I said so," has many disguises, especially when discussing faith. It can look like the following: "Because your grandma wants you to be baptized," "Because the Pope says so," "Because that's what the church says," "Because that's just what Catholics do," or "Because you have to be confirmed to get married in the Catholic Church." All of these responses provide unsatisfactory, empty answers for children growing in faith.

The words "Because I said so" do not make for bad parenting. At times, it's okay to respond this way. In fact, it's a right every parent has earned. Sometimes we say these things because the question defies explanation at a child's level of understanding. As a second-grade CCD teacher, I was once asked by a student, "How did Noah keep the penguins cold and the lions warm on the ark?"

The student was disappointed by my answer. I explained we have to trust and have faith that God can do anything, but we don't always know *how* God does what he can. After much discussion, this second-grader eventually received the response, "Because the Bible says so."

If you have ever been around a three-year-old, you know there is *no answer* to the question "Why?" that will ever satisfy their insatiable curiosity or their need to hone their negotiation skills. Perhaps every parent has had this conversation with his or her three-year-old:

> Child: "Why do we have to go to church?"
> Parent: "We don't *have* to go to church we *get* to go to church."
> Child: "Why?"
> Parent: "To spend time with Jesus."
> Child: "Why do we need to spend time with Jesus?"
> Parent: "To praise Him and thank Him."
> Child: "Why do we have to thank Him?"
> Parent (with exasperation): "Because He died for us."
> Child: "Why did He die for us?"
> Parent: "So we could live forever in heaven."
> Child: "Why does Jesus want us to live in heaven?"
> Parent: "So we can be happy."
> Child: "Why?"
> Parent: "Because."
> Child: "Because why?"
> Parent: "Because I said so."

What I have learned as a parent is that often when I say, "Because I said so," I am truly saying, "Because I love you." So, "Because I said so, *and* I love you" is the more accurate response, especially when talking about faith. I constantly promise my children two things: I will make mistakes as a parent, but every decision I make will be made out of love. If parents didn't love their children, they wouldn't *make* them go to church because they said so. Yes, parents love their children so much they want them to share in communion with Christ because they are vastly aware of the joy it can bring to them.

When Jesus became flesh and died for each of us, sinners that we are, He did it because He loves us. Period. This is always Jesus's response, whether we deserve it or not. One thing Jesus came to teach us is forgiveness. Perhaps today, Jesus might have been found saying, "You should forgive *because I said so*." So technically, "Because *God* said so," should also be enough of an answer. However, as I so humbly learned from the second-grader inquiring about Noah, to sufficiently *feed* inquisitive, and even suspicious, children this answer alone can be a disservice to their spiritual growth. Parents have a responsibility to learn the real answers to the "why" questions in order to nurture and grow their own faith as well as the faith of their children.

When I was a young adult, my non-Catholic friends would ask me why I dipped my hands in holy water as I entered church. My response was always, "Because that's just what Catholics do." I could sense their disappointment when that was all I had to offer by way of explanation. I also noticed this empty response usually ended our discussion. How unfortunate for me I did not understand that I performed this action to remind me of my baptism. Today, if someone were to ask me why Catholics dip their hands in holy water, there is likely to be a long discussion that follows. I have a small holy water font in my living room. I use it occasionally on my way out of my home to remind me I belong to God's family and I am called to serve Him through my baptism. That becomes my mission for the day, and it makes all the difference. My family thinks I'm a little crazy for having the holy water font in my house, but it has helped my children be absolutely sure of why Catholics dip their hands in holy water.

Consider the common query, "Why do Catholics have to go to confession?"

Now consider the following answer: "You *get* to go to confession because God loves you so much, He wants to give you His grace to help you enjoy the kingdom of heaven and be surrounded by His love forever. He gave us this beautiful gift to help us and to remind us of His presence in our lives. In not keeping the Lord's commands or sinning against the Lord, we offend Him and Christians everywhere; we fail to glorify the Father. When we sin, we hurt Christ (someone who loves us so much He gave His life for each of us). Christ came to show us the way to the Father. He showed us how to forgive and asked us to follow His example. Confession gives us the chance to reconcile with Him and all our brothers and sisters in Christ through the authority Christ handed down to the priest" (see John 20:21–23). When they are given a more complete answer, it makes it easier for Catholics to appreciate and participate in the gift of reconciliation.

The phrase, "Because I said so" is designed to *end* a discussion. In order to grow in our faith, we must *engage* in discussion. The NFCYM data reports that 84 percent of Catholic teens say religion is important in daily life. Knowing how important faith is to our Catholic children, don't use "Because I said so" for the big questions. Save it for the likes of: "Why can't I have thirty of my friends over for a sleepover tonight?"

---

"And be kind to one another, compassionate, forgiving one another as God has forgiven you in Christ" (Eph. 4:32).

# PART II
# Commit

*Let's Decide If You Are Ready to Start Growing*

☙

# 6
# Are You a Chicken or a Pig?

I once read the quote by Ken Blanchard, "There is a difference between interest and commitment. If you are interested in something, you do it when it is convenient. When you are committed, you accept no excuses, only results."

Later, I received this message a bit more clearly in another quote that reads, "Consider the matter of bacon and eggs: the chicken makes a contribution, the pig makes a commitment."

I like the chicken and the pig analogy because it is tangible. I can see it. I can touch it. I can even eat it! When I reflect on this breakfast meal, I realize it is also very relevant to my faith. It helps me recognize my commitment—or lack of commitment—to my faith. Do you have the commitment of the chicken or the pig for growing Catholic children in your home? In essence, are you *interested* in growing Catholic children or are you *committed* to it?

The first step in growing Catholics or growing as a Catholic yourself is to make a real commitment to it. Think about the baptismal promises you will make or have made on behalf of your children. Growing Catholics is not something Jesus expects us to do only when it is convenient. Look at the example he gave us. Jesus's commitment to his covenant with us resulted in his death. Thank goodness He didn't say, "It really isn't convenient for me to die on the cross today; I have another engagement."

Look at the following examples to help determine your level of commitment to your faith.

- Do you pray daily, read the Bible, or talk about your faith with others?
- Do you receive the sacrament of reconciliation and practice forgiveness regularly?
- Do you find a Mass to attend when traveling or vacationing?
- Do you follow all the teachings of the church rather than just those that suit you?
- Do you serve others in your community or volunteer at church?

The list could go on and on, but with these examples, you simply need to ask yourself, "Am I committed to my faith, or am I just interested in it?" Is it enough for you to say, "I am a Catholic," or is it more important that you have a relationship with Christ and continually grow in your faith?

During my first two years of college, my answer to each of the questions in the list above was, "No." I continued to tell others I was Catholic, but I clearly did not have Christ in my life. So, when I was in a painful relationship, I could not share in the peace that comes from forgiveness. Instead, I experienced great pain and showed anger. When I suffered from depression, I did not know the hope that God can give those who trust in Him because I was unfamiliar with the Bible.

Today, I can proudly answer, "Yes," to all the questions in the list, and I do have peace and hope in my life. For example, instead of hating my enemies, I pray for them as Jesus says to do: "But I say to you, love your enemies, and pray for those who persecute you" (Matt. 5:44). I have to admit when I started this practice, I was a bit inexperienced. My early prayers sounded like, "God, teach that person a lesson for me," or "God, please make them be nice or see things my way." However, because I am now committed to reading the Bible, I know how to pray the way Jesus asks me to pray. My prayer today is: "God, please be with my enemy, show them Your love, and give them the strength to do Your will. Amen." This miraculous transformation all started with a commitment—a commitment I made over twenty years ago as I was considering the baptism of my first child.

As you consider your commitment to the Eucharistic feast, for example, notice what Jesus says in the parable of the great feast found in the Gospel of Luke (14:15–24):

> One by one [those invited] all began to excuse themselves …
> "I have purchased a field and must examine it …"
> "I have purchased five yoke of oxen and am on my way to evaluate them …"
> "I have just married a woman and cannot come."

And the parable concludes with the master saying, "For I tell you, none of those men who were invited will taste my dinner." Jesus is clearly looking for a commitment, just as he demonstrated.

If you are committed to faith, your children will know it. Unfortunately, if you are only *interested* in faith, they will know this too. Your children have undoubtedly "pushed the envelope" a time or two—parents of teenagers especially know the meaning of this phrase. Take the matter of an evening curfew. If you are *interested* in them being home by 11:00 PM, they probably will not get punished for arriving at 11:20 PM. If you are *committed* to them being home by 11:00 PM, you begin calling parents and friends to locate your child at 11:01 PM and a consequence will likely be imposed. See the difference? I guarantee you children recognize the difference. If you do not discipline a child for being late for curfew, it is hard to correct a child when they go against other "suggestions" you may offer, such as going to church. If parents find it important for their children to arrive home at a reasonable time, they should also have similar commitments to faith, which will provide them with everlasting life. It may seem simplistic to make this comparison, but it is not. One (the curfew) just happens to be more tangible than the other (God's love, faith, and everlasting life).

Children know how to push buttons. They know which schoolteachers allow them to turn assignments in late and which ones do not. What do your children know about you as a teacher of the faith? As a Catholic parent, which of your buttons are negotiable and which buttons are not? Going to church is not optional in our home;

therefore, on Sunday mornings, I don't get the question, "Do we have to go to church?"

What commitments are you making, and what examples are you setting? The NFCYM data shows only 36 percent of Catholic teens and 42 percent of their parents attend Mass at least once a week. Clearly, this national figure does not represent a commitment to the sacrament of Eucharist. Instead, it demonstrates the Catholic Church may have more *chickens*, who are only interested in Mass when it is convenient. In other words, a majority of Catholic parents and teens are not making a *commitment* to their faith. I challenge you to be like the "pig" in the quotation at the beginning of this chapter. I challenge you to be part of the privileged and joyful minority who are truly committed to their faith.

In my life, I have been both the chicken and the pig. Being the chicken was unequivocally easier, but being the pig is much more fulfilling. Today, more than twenty years after writing that college paper against Catholicism, I proudly profess a lot of growth. This growth came because of commitments—a commitment by God to keep His covenant of salvation, a commitment by my parents at my baptism, a commitment by my family and religion teachers to reinforce my faith, and finally, a personal commitment by me. Although it seems strange to say it, I am no longer interested in my faith; I am committed to it.

---

"Commit your way to the Lord; trust that God will act" (Ps. 37:5).

# 7
# What Chocolate Taught Me

I used to be addicted to chocolate. In fact, you could say I was *committed* to chocolate to the extent that I would get up in the middle of the night to make a batch of chocolate cookies to satisfy a chocolate craving. This is not something I am very proud of, but it now helps me to understand my priorities in life. This behavior becomes my litmus test for determining what should be important to me. For example, if I evaluated my chocolate addiction, I could conclude the following: I was willing to get up in the middle of the night for chocolate. Chocolate had never died for my sins, and (as much joy as I received from eating chocolate) it had never shown me God's love. Yet, I would sacrifice something as important as sleep to obtain it. On the other hand, God loves me so much that He *has* sacrificed for me, and that is what I *should* be getting up in the middle of the night for—to pray to God, to be with Jesus in adoration, or to read the Bible. Spending time with God is what can give me a share in the kingdom on earth and in heaven. Eating chocolate, quite simply, will not. That is what I learned from chocolate.

Identify the addictions or obstacles that keep you from sharing faith or growing in your faith. Perhaps it is sports, television, food, gossip, or feelings of inadequacy. Whatever it is, determine if this addiction is bringing you toward a closer relationship with God or keeping you from that relationship. It is not bad to play sports or watch television, but these activities must not be done to the exclusion of spending time with our faith. What keeps you from sharing faith in the home? What steps can you take to remove these obstacles and addictions and make time for faith?

Our addictions and faith do not have to be mutually exclusive; sometimes, addictions can be used to strengthen faith. If music is your addiction, you can listen to Christian music or you can share God's love with others by singing at Mass. Instead of watching reality television, you could watch religious programming. In the movie *Chariots of Fire*, the main character is a very gifted runner who has strong Jewish faith. He uses his gift of running to help spread the word of God, and he is so committed to his faith that he will not run on the Sabbath—not even for an Olympic preliminary race and a chance to win a gold medal. For some, this seems absurd or totally unreasonable. Some may even rationalize, "God would understand; He would want him to win the gold medal. Everybody else is doing it; it's no big deal."

It is hard to imagine giving up something like an Olympic gold medal, but this athlete clearly understood the long-lasting joy of sharing God's love over the temporary joy he would receive from winning a gold medal. This athlete demonstrated a commitment to his faith, and his "reward in heaven will be great" (Matt. 5:12). His actions certainly were a powerful way to share faith and evangelize to those around him. Celebrated professional tennis player Martina Navratilova once said, "The moment of victory is much too short to live for that and nothing else." Apart from Christ's victory over death through His resurrection, Ms. Navratilova's words speak volumes to this idea of commitment and priorities.

As a confirmation coordinator, I was once told by a parent, "If I have to choose between basketball and confirmation class for my daughter, I will choose basketball every time." She was astounded that I didn't share her commitment. She called a meeting with me to see if I could fit confirmation around her daughter's sports schedule. I was challenging her to do the exact opposite. As a former athlete and the mother of athletes, I understood the enjoyment that comes from watching and participating in sports activities. However, I shared with this parent how I had taken my children from sports practices to attend religious events under coaches' threats of reduced playing time, and she looked at me in disbelief. I admit that the pressure to go along with the coaches' priorities was huge, and this was a very hard thing to do.

I winced at the pain on my children's faces as I made these decisions. Each time we challenged coaches, they adjusted their standpoint. No playing time was lost, and we noticed this pattern year after year.

A few short years later, when my son was making the decision to give up playing baseball, he told me, "Imagine what a better person I would be if all the time and energy I spent with this coach and these practices were spent on my faith."

The joy I received from that statement puts the memory of the home run my son hit on Mother's Day to shame. He and I learned that the happiness received from athletic success to the exclusion of faith cannot compare to the joy found in having a relationship with Jesus. Unfortunately, this is not what society or athletic coaches always teach our children today. I truly pray for everyone to one day know the difference.

My investments in sports and chocolate have generated a small fraction of the benefits my investment in faith has given me. A few years ago, my children challenged me to give up sleep by rising earlier in the morning as a Lenten sacrifice. They knew this was a sacrifice for me because I enjoy sleep and am definitely not a morning person. Every other Monday, I began getting up at 4:15 AM to spend an hour in the adoration chapel, and over five years later, I can witness to you that the benefits of my hour in adoration far outweigh the sacrifice of sleep I make. This is always the case when we sacrifice for Christ. If the martyrs and saints are my example of true sacrifice, I still have a long way to go, but making time for my faith has been instrumental to my growth.

Today, parents seem to want children to have everything, experience everything, and be the best at everything. They want them to be on the best sports team, or have the best music or dance instructors. They are willing to commit many dollars and a lot of time to these causes. What a wonderful world it would be if they shared this commitment to giving their child the best of religion and faith too. Just as the best coaches and a lot of time practicing may provide children success in sports or the arts, practice and commitment will provide them success in obtaining a life of joy in Christ. This is the best commitment we can make to our children.

Your goal as a parent is to get your children to heaven. It is not to make them a lot of money or to get them the fanciest job, house, car, etc., or all the material things they need.

You must prepare them for a life (and eternal life) with Christ.

---

"Do not store up for yourselves treasures on earth, where moth and decay destroy, and thieves break in and steal. But store up treasures in heaven, where neither moth nor decay destroy, nor thieves break in and steal. For where your treasure is, there also will your heart be" (Matt. 6:19–21).

# 8
# Stepping Up to the Plate

My son has played baseball since he was two years old, and I am a fan of the sport at the professional level. As a result, I have logged many innings enjoying America's pastime. I even enjoy watching the many gyrations batters go through prior to obtaining their final stance at home plate in preparation for a pitch. If you have never witnessed this, just imagine baseball players digging in their baseball cleats as if to grab hold of the batter's box with their feet to prepare for what is about to come. They know the pitch will be full of power, and they want to be ready for it. To me, this image says a lot about our faith journey. God can be so powerful when we let Him work in our lives and actually follow His will, so we better dig in and grab hold for what He will "pitch" us.

As parents to Catholic children, the phrase "step up to the plate" means to get in the game, be an active participant, and don't back down. Be committed to swinging the bat. Be committed to *growing* Catholic children. The Catholic Church recognizes that parents have "the first responsibility for the education of their children in the faith, prayer, and all the virtues" (CCC 2252). It goes on further to call the family the "domestic church" or Ecclesia Domestica (CCC 1656). At the sacrament of baptism, parents are asked during the rite of their children to "make it your constant care to bring him (her) up in the practice of the faith." They are told, "You are accepting the responsibility of training him (her) in the practice of the faith." It asks the godparents if they are "ready to help the parents of this child in their duty." The church does not say, "Let a priest do it, or a Catholic school, or the Bible, or the Pope." These are all excellent tools to assist both you and your children; however, ultimately, it is the parents who must step up to the plate.

For about ten years, I taught CCD (Confraternity of Christian Doctrine), parish religion classes for public school children. I have had students tell me, "I don't have to learn prayers because I go to public school," or "I don't have to go to confession because I go to public school now." Although I never expressed similar sentiments as a child, it did appear my church or religion class was my faith. I was a child whose family did not share much faith, so the only place I really received lessons about faith or read the Bible was at school. In essence, my school was my faith. Although I was taught much about my religion, it was not being reinforced at home and it was clearly not enough. Perhaps school is the only place many children learn about faith. Perhaps school is the only place they even *practice* their faith. Recall from the previous chapter that the majority of Catholic teens and parents do not attend weekly Mass. A commitment to faith is a commitment to the Mass.

For several years while I was in college, I was among the majority who didn't attend Mass on Sunday. I justified this decision because the "building" did nothing for me. I believed I did not need to partake in the empty motions and rote prayers the Mass offered, nor did I care to be "brainwashed" by the messages. What I didn't realize was I wasn't just removing the *building* from my life; I was removing the people, including Christ. I had to learn that it is the *people* who are the church, not the bricks and the mortar. The Catechism of the Catholic Church (CCC 752) tells us, "The Church is the people God has gathered in the whole world." It does not define the church as the *buildings* he has gathered.

Today, I am back in the building church, and it helps me to surround myself with the church that is the people of God. Each person in that building is being a witness to their faith as I sit alongside them. The people in that building—Christ, the priests and religious, and the people present—all remind me of my apostolic mission and the importance of faith and my faith family. I also learned the motions have meaning and are not empty, and although I don't call the messages brainwashing today, I would argue our world would be a better place if we were all brainwashed on the messages of love, hope, peace, and forgiveness heard at Mass. Learning these things helped me make the commitment to attend church. All parents need to make this same commitment, but they must also commit to being the church *outside* the building. Christ must be seen in our world through the people of God, both clergy and laity.

So, how can we be the church in the world? We are the church when we share Christ's love with those around us. We can be the church when we help others in need, or when we are kind to a stranger. We can be the church when we make pilgrimages to Washington DC to participate in a pro-life march. My children have volunteered with me to prepare and serve meals at our local Salvation Army; they have been Special Olympics volunteers alongside me. We have attended masses on important days that are not holy days of obligation. In addition, there are many things we do as a family that help us to be the church outside of the building. Each time we ask forgiveness or seek forgiveness from each other, we are building the Kingdom of God. In our homes, parents are the church when they continue the work of Christ by teaching children the faith.

One year, I challenged my children to prepare a prayer service for the family during Advent. Each family member was to take a week and lead the prayer service. I went first at the family's request to give everyone ideas on activities. One of my activities included a period of personal faith sharing. It was a bit uncomfortable for the children to share, and I remember feeling a bit disappointed at their unease. After all, we had talked about faith and religion many times. At the conclusion of the prayer service, I thought I would not get them to participate the following week. Later, I had a conversation with my eldest daughter about my concern, and she said, "Mom, I want to do this because when you have your religious discussions with Brian [her older brother], I always want to listen in on the conversation." We finished the prayer services, and it became a growing experience for us all. I also came to realize that I talked *to* my children about faith or I talked *at* them, but I never really *shared* with them. I often think of what I would have missed out on if I had not gone through that initial uncomfortable experience. I may not have known that my daughter was hungry to learn more. I would have missed out on some awesome family prayer services, and I would have missed an opportunity to grow myself.

At the building church, we are left with the words, "Go in peace to love and serve the Lord." That means, "Go be the church in the world." So, make the commitment to go to the building church on Sundays and holy days, and then commit to *being* the church the other six days. Start by being the church in your family. Begin by praying together, studying scripture together, serving others together, forgiving each other, and loving each other. It may be a bit uncomfortable at first, like my family Advent prayer service, but I guarantee you will not be disappointed. If you become the church in your family and are disappointed, I will refund you the cost of this book. Pray for the courage to try something new, and trust that God will take care of things. I challenged my family during Advent many years ago; now I challenge you. If nothing else, step up to the plate, chose one specific way to be the church at home today.

# 9
# Homeschooling

It seems much attention has been given to homeschooled children. They win national geography contests, spelling bees, and the like, making homeschooling seem very effective. I believe all children are homeschooled. Parents help children with homework. They teach children how to belong to a family, how to have manners, how to budget an allowance or do chores, etc. Parents may even teach reading, 'riting, and 'rithmatic at home to support what is being taught at school. In the same way, Catholic schools teach religion to supplement what is being taught in the home. Parents, working together with teachers, help children to be more successful.

It came to my attention in my role as director of religious education that some Catholic parents believe if their child is attending a religion class (forty minutes a day or an hour each week), they are meeting their baptismal obligation of bringing their children up in the faith. This is a very misguided notion. From my personal experience in teaching religion, whether it was a weekly CCD class or in a daily Catholic school classroom, I am never surprised to discover my best religion students, unequivocally, are the students who are being taught religion at home.

If my Catholic upbringing has taught me anything, it is that faith is *caught* not taught. I *caught* the devotion to Eucharist from my father by his enduring example. His example made it easy for my school to teach me to remember the Sabbath and make it holy. To the contrary,

I found it more difficult to understand the value of saying the Rosary as *taught* to me in school because it was not shown to me at home. Catholic schools and parish CCD programs have a tremendous value in helping to grow Catholic children; however, these resources cannot be seen as alternatives to parents teaching and modeling faith in the home. It is the role of Catholic education to *support* what is being taught and modeled in the home, not vice versa. Both resources absolutely must work together. Children will learn more about the Eucharist in the classroom when they attend Mass with their families each Sunday.

At the age of twenty-two, I was preparing to have my first child baptized. It was during this preparation I was reminded of how little I knew about the faith I was about to commit to teaching. I was about to make a baptismal promise to "accept the responsibility of training [my child] in the practice of the faith." This was a promise I took very seriously, especially since I was making it to God—in front of a priest and a church full of witnesses! I asked myself, "Am I really prepared to make this commitment? Does this innocent child deserve to understand this lifelong commitment I am making for him?" I decided the answer was a resounding, "Yes!"

Because of my experiences being raised Catholic, I knew what it felt like to not understand my faith. I knew how painful it was to not be able to defend my faith when asked about it. I knew how hard it was for me to relearn and get the answers I needed to grow spiritually. I knew the suffering I experienced when I had neglected my relationship with Christ. I did not want my child to experience these same pains. I knew my child would ask the same questions I asked as a Catholic. I knew my child would be tested by others about his faith. I decided not to perpetuate my Catholic experience with my child. I was now committed to *growing* a Catholic, which also meant I was committed to my own conversion and growth. I was committed to *homeschooling* my child in faith.

Of my three children, I have one who excels in math but struggled with reading early on, one who has math anxiety but is great at writing, and one who is a self-proclaimed reading maniac. God blesses each child with unique gifts. Being a parent responsible for growing three children has taught me to modify the way I teach, discipline, and share faith with each of them. Each of their faith journeys has been different and has peaked at different times in their lives. Because I know them better than any classroom teacher, priest, or Pope could know them, my role as a teacher of faith becomes far more important. I know right were they are in their growth.

For several years, I assisted with confirmation preparation classes. Some students in the classroom are ready to challenge their faith during these classes, while some would clearly rather be somewhere else. Some have had significant faith experiences already, and some are, in their own words, only in class because their parents said they would buy them a car if they received the sacrament. Much like me at my confirmation, some are simply going through the motions. Each student has a different life experience and unique faith story. I would be fooling myself to believe I can reach all thirty to seventy students at any given time with a particular teaching activity. If I reach one, it is considered a success. With those odds, I explain to parents of those to be confirmed and their sponsors the importance of their role during this preparation time. They know their child and their child's faith story well enough to know how to encourage and challenge them to grow. No matter how well I might get to know these students, I don't have the whole picture.

I am thankful for the support I receive from my faith community and the Catholic school. On many occasions, these two resources working together have provided me with stories of growth. When my youngest daughter asked me if she could take a nap at Mass, I asked, "Why?"

She replied very matter-of-factly, "Jesus isn't at Mass. He's taking a nap."

Upon further inquiry, I discovered that in teaching the story of creation, her kindergarten teacher explained how God *rested* on the seventh day. The school taught creation; as a parent, I supported the teaching by clarifying a misunderstanding. Had I not been homeschooling my child in faith, the conversation may have never come up and an opportunity to grow could have been missed.

On a recent camping trip, I was pleased to learn that an outdoor Catholic Mass was offered at our campsite. I was excited to offer this experience to my family. I had the Mass times and wanted to surprise them with the outdoor Mass where tree stumps served as pews. On Sunday morning, I received the information that the Catholic masses were seasonal and would not begin for a few more weeks. In a panic,

I truly did with due diligence look for a Mass but resigned myself to the fact that we may have to actually miss a Sunday Mass until the voice of my youngest daughter came from the back of our recreational vehicle saying, "We are not going to break the third commandment." Needless to say, we unhitched everything, drove to the nearest town, and randomly drove to a gas station for directions only to discover we were exactly one block from a Catholic church. We parked a large RV in a crowded neighborhood and arrived at a Mass just as the opening song was finishing up. My daughter was studying the commandments at school. The lesson supported our need to attend; we supported the lesson by honoring the commandment.

As you can see from the camping example, I clearly understand and appreciate how children can help catechize their parents. As a Catholic schoolteacher, I often assign parent homework just for this purpose. Parent homework can be anything that engages parents and their children in a conversation about their faith. Homework could be to tell your child the story of his or her baptism, say a decade of the Rosary with your child, or let your child quiz you on Christmas trivia questions. The idea began over fifteen years ago with a phone call from my sister, who was looking for help with one of her children's religion assignments. The assignment was to explain the symbolism behind the signs of the cross Catholics make on their forehead, lips, and heart prior to the reading of the Gospel. None of us knew the answer. After much research and many phone calls, we arrived at the answer. We spent so much time researching it that I have never forgotten the answer.[3] Now that's teamwork.

So even though my children have religion classes, I am proud to profess I have homeschooled all of them in the subject of faith. That's my job. If God came to your front door and showed you the exact steps needed to guarantee your child gets to heaven, I pray you would not withhold that information from your child and say, "I think they are learning that next week in religion class." I hope you would stop at nothing to give your child these steps. Isn't knowledge of eternal life important enough for you to be sure they understand it by teaching it to them yourself? Just to set the record straight, God has provided you with these steps to get your child to heaven; it is called the Bible. If you

---

3   The answer: prior to the reading of the Gospel, we ask God to let his Word be on our minds, on our lips, and in our hearts.

do not have one, go purchase a New American Bible or a Catholic Study Bible today, and be prepared to learn more in coming chapters.

I have seen in my life how having faith only taught at school kept me from growing. I have also seen how home and parish working together has provided opportunities for growth. For this reason, I pray you will get involved in your parish, learn what your children are learning about faith by asking them, and homeschool them on the subjects of faith, even if your child's religion class or church already teaches it. It all starts with conversation. This conversation may be new, awkward, or inconvenient, but a conversation with children about faith is never wasted. If you are not convinced, ask yourself this: How much time do I spend talking to others about non-faith matters, and how productive is all that conversation? If you can concede that at least five minutes a day is wasted on frivolous conversation, then what do you have to lose by devoting five minutes of conversation with your child to the subject of faith?

For your parent homework, I assign you to have a five-minute conversation with your child about your faith. Be prepared to be surprised.

# PART III
# **Pray**

*Begin Your Conversion
with Conversation*

☙

# 10
# In God We Trust

Once the commitment is made and the addictions are removed, the *only* place to start on the road to growth is prayer. As I mentioned earlier, as I was growing up, my family prayed and attended Mass every Sunday. I prayed at Catholic school, and I prayed alone at times. For the most part, my prayer was somewhat like going through the motions. In order to grow in faith and be a person of continual conversion (growth), I had to be in conversation with God. I had to truly become a prayerful person. Catholics need to be prayerful people beyond the Sunday Eucharist. They must make time to talk to God and listen to Him each day. Prayer transforms your life. I challenge all the skeptics to try to prove me wrong. This has been the single most important step in my journey, which is why it comes before all others. Make prayer a part of your every day and watch it make a difference.

As a former skeptic, I found myself struggling with my job and was trying to discern whether or not I should leave my current position. I consulted a priest. All of the steps I learned while getting my bachelor's degree in business for problem-solving, assessing situations, and brainstorming had failed me. I will never forget the advice the priest gave me, nor will I forget my response to his advice. He told me to pray about the issue, and I am ashamed to admit I was disappointed with the suggestion. I thought, "I need a real (secular) solution; I need some concrete action to resolve this issue." My disappointment came because I did not truly understand the power of prayer at that point in my life, nor was I willing to trust in God's answer to my prayer. However, since the advice came from a priest and I had been taught by the nuns in elementary school to be obedient, I prayed. I began praying rather unenthusiastically because I saw it as an obligation not a blessing. Finally, however, I began to really pray and truly trust. A few Sundays later, as I entered church for Sunday Eucharist, I prayed for God to send me a message in the readings or the homily that day at Mass. I had been at my job for three years and felt I was spinning my wheels, that my work was "fruitless." Imagine my surprise at the reading, which was from the Gospel of Luke (13:7–8) which says,

> He said to the gardener, "For three years now I have come in search of fruit on this fig tree but have found none. [So] cut it down. Why should it exhaust the soil?"
> He said to him in reply, "Sir, leave it for this year also, and I shall cultivate the ground around it and fertilize it; it may bear fruit in the future. If not you can cut it down."

Needless to say, I got the message. God doesn't always answer this way, but apparently, I needed this at the time. I continued to pray, and I have never looked back since.

As I was growing up, my mother was a big fan of the phrase, "If you want something done right, you have to do it yourself." I found it to be true so often that this phrase became my mantra. I knew I could trust in myself; I didn't know how much I could trust in others. After all, I had been let down by others before, so why risk it? Plus, I liked the control this gave me over situations. The problem was that I became so dependent on myself that my trust in me came at the exclusion of my trust in God. I was still a believer in God, but I seemed unwilling to let Him handle things since I was doing such a good job at it. In hindsight, I realize how absurd and arrogant that notion was. I was unwilling to trust the God who created day and night, the trees, the waters, the stars, the sun, the moon, etc.—*all out of nothing.* This is the God who created me (Gen. 1:27), who knew me before I was formed in the womb (Jer. 1:5), who knows what I need before I ask him (Matt. 6:8), and who loves me so much he gave his only son (John 3:16). I had the nerve to not trust this God? Wrong.

God had a big lesson for me on trust and control. There is an old

Yiddish proverb that says, "Man plans and God laughs." I had plans, and I had trust in my plans, but I was human and my plans eventually failed. I made some bad decisions and could not avoid the consequences of those decisions. I had no one to blame but myself. The consequences of these bad decisions seemed too much for me to handle on my own. I got so low I finally had to consider, "Do I need someone else to help me do it right?" Furthermore, I had to consider, "Whom can I trust?"

The answer was as plain as the words on the dollar bill: "In God We Trust." Scripture told me, "Better to take refuge in the Lord, than to put one's trust in mortals" (Ps. 118:8). I was ready to trust in God's will, and I was ready to pray the way Jesus prayed at Gethsemane: "But not what I will but what you will" (Mark 14:36).

Now that I am in constant conversation with Christ through prayer, I see the difference it makes. Recently, I was on my way to give a presentation on the topic of prayer. I was running behind schedule, so I decided to drive a bit over the speed limit. On my drive to the event, the proverbial "little old lady" pulled out in front of my speeding vehicle and proceeded to travel fifteen miles an hour *under* the speed limit. I wish I was exaggerating this fact. There was no opportunity for me to pass her car, and I am ashamed to admit I was not very pleasant or Christian in my mood at that moment. Perhaps you have had a similar experience. I gripped the steering wheel tighter. I spoke out loud to myself about how this lady should not be driving and why she should have waited to pull onto the street after I had passed. I then noticed she was weaving a bit in her lane, which gave me cause to speak out loud again about how this driver should not even have a license. My blood was boiling, my muscles were tense, and my heart was angry. Then I remembered I was driving to give a talk about prayer, so I prayed. I began by thanking Jesus for putting this lady in front of me to remind me that no matter how busy I get, I have to make time for Him. Then I began praying for the safe arrival of this driver. At this point, I noticed my heart had quit racing; my loud voice had become soft; my heart had been filled with compassion, peace, and love; and I had even begun to laugh to myself out loud about the irony of the situation. As you can see, prayer did not change God; it changed me.

I truly witnessed the power of a simple prayer and was reminded that when praying is the last thing I want to do, it is usually the time I need it most. In addition, I received a bonus in that God gave me the perfect introduction to my presentation in the telling of this story. How awesome is this God to be able to make all those things fall into place? That's who I trust!

People have let me down and continue to do so, but God never has. If I don't get my prayer answered the way I think is right, I trust God always gives me the answer I need.

---

"Blessed is the man who trusts in the Lord, whose hope is the Lord. He is like a tree planted beside the waters that stretches out its roots to the stream: It fears not the heat when it comes, its leaves stay green; In the year of drought it shows no distress, but still bears fruit" (Jer. 17:7–8).

# 11
# Broccoli, Shrimp, and the Rosary

It is impossible for me to educate you about everything you need to know about prayer in these pages—there are so many different ways to pray—but the best advice I can give is to just do it. I'll never forget attending a church meeting where it was announced that the pastor was going to be late. The gentleman leading the meeting glanced at the agenda, saw that an opening prayer was listed as item one, and said, "We'll skip that since Father is not here." No one spoke up, so I volunteered to lead the prayer. I was discouraged that this group of church leaders felt they couldn't pray, but it made me aware of two realities about Catholics and prayer. Too many Catholics are uncomfortable leading prayer because it is not a part of their everyday conversation, and many Catholics also reserve prayer for religious leaders.

When I worked in the rectory of a church, my husband used to send me to work with prayer intentions to give to Father. He used to joke that God gives the priests' prayers more attention, but we both know that God listens to all prayers, and priests do not have a special, direct line to God for their prayers. Furthermore, priests do not have a monopoly on leading prayers before a church meeting, as in the example above; they simply have more practice at it. Everyone can pray, and everyone should be comfortable doing it whether it is a spontaneous prayer or a rote prayer. There are many resources on prayer, but allow me to share the following story as a source for guiding you as you search and practice.

When I was young, I could not stand the sight of broccoli. It repulsed me because I had actually tasted it and was sickened. As a teenager, I could actually tolerate the green vegetable if it were cooked and smothered in cheese sauce. Now that I am over forty years old, I can eat this green stuff right off the stalk, raw. On the other hand, I tasted shrimp as a child, as a teenager, as a twenty-year-old, thirty-year-old, and forty-year-old and have never liked it. I have sampled shrimp boiled, broiled, breaded, fried, etc., and will probably continue to sample it because I feel I'm missing out on something. It seems everybody loves shrimp.

Then there is the Rosary. I mentioned earlier my family didn't pray the Rosary, and my experience with this devotion was limited to praying it at Catholic school. The truth is I really didn't understand this prayer, so I wasn't really a fan of it. This is not a sin. For years, I misunderstood the little old ladies reciting the Rosary in church. I went so far as to judge them by saying, "How can that be a prayer? They are merely mumbling the words without much care or thought." So I thought, until one evening when I felt desperate for a prayer and words failed me. My usual conversation with God wasn't working for me on this night. I remember saying to myself, "If these little old ladies have so much faith in it, it's worth a shot. I've got nothing to lose." Fortunately, I had a great book on the meditations of the Rosary to guide me. I needed it because I truly did not know the prayers or the mysteries of the Rosary at that time in my life.

That night, I prayed the Rosary, meditating on the Sorrowful Mysteries, and I finally got it. I chose the Sorrowful Mysteries because I was feeling sorry for myself that things didn't seem to be going my way in life. All I had to do was begin my meditation on the second Sorrowful Mystery, the Scourging at the Pillar, to finally realize what a beautiful prayer this was. I started thinking about Jesus being beaten, spat upon, kicked, and whipped for me and realized that my problem was so trivial compared to that sacrifice. I felt ashamed of my self-pity. I understood in that moment that God was giving me exactly what I needed. I found the comfort I was looking for, and I was meditating so hard on the mysteries I don't even recall saying the Hail Mary and the Our Father. I'm guessing if someone had walked by, they may have said, "How can that be a prayer? She is merely mumbling the words without much care or thought."

The Rosary was like broccoli for me. I wasn't ready to like it until this moment in my life. Thank goodness I kept trying. Had I not tried broccoli as I got older, imagine all the great food dishes I may have missed. Had I not revisited the Rosary, the peace and joy it offers would be missing in my life today.

There are two lessons here. First, if you're not a fan of the Rosary, that is okay. There is no wrong way to pray. There are many different types of prayers and many methods for praying. If you are praying with an open heart, you are doing it the "right way." Your right way may include a favorite time of day to pray or a favorite place to pray. If you are comfortable with adoration, do it. If you enjoy rote prayer, keep praying those prayers. Discover your right way, and pray the way you like.

The second lesson in the broccoli, shrimp, and Rosary story is to keep sampling the many ways of lifting your heart in prayer in order to continue growing. If I had never sampled shrimp, how could I profess I don't like shrimp with confidence? This is why I always challenge those who say they don't need prayer to prove me wrong by praying. To truly find what method works for you, you must experiment with an open heart and revisit various methods when necessary. At different times in our lives, our needs for prayer may change, just like our taste buds.

You may never be a fan of the Rosary, like I may never be a fan of shrimp, but don't give up easily. You must listen and converse with God in some way. Without question, prayerful people are spiritual people, and spiritual people are content people. It is hard to be in conversation with God and still want to yell at a little old lady driving too slowly. Growing in faith requires you to become a prayerful person. In the words of Saint Paul to the Thessalonians, "Pray without ceasing" (1 Thess. 5:17).

---

"… his disciples said to him, 'Lord, teach us to pray …'
"He said to them, 'When you pray, say: Father, hallowed be your name, your kingdom come. Give us each day our daily bread and forgive us our sins for we ourselves forgive everyone in debt to us, and do not subject us to the final test'" (Luke 11:1–4).

# 12
# Will You Be My Friend?

The most important part of my spiritual growth was prayer. I prayed, and I prayed, and I prayed a lot. So much so that I now feel I have a personal relationship with Jesus. How awesome it is to call Jesus your friend. This title of *friend* is not reserved for those who walked alongside Jesus during his life on earth. He longs for this relationship with all His people. When I was younger, I thought of God as a judge sitting up in Heaven keeping track of all the good and bad things I did. I envisioned Him making a list and checking it twice. This was a very distant relationship and the type of relationship Christ came into this world to change. Today, through prayer alone, I have come to call Him "friend," and Jesus tells all of us, "I have called you friends" (John 15:15).

Think of the first friend you might call on the telephone if you received some good news, the first you would call when you were angry or upset, and the first you might call for encouragement and support. Chances are you would call the same person in all three incidents. Now, substitute that person's name with the name Jesus. I started my relationship by making Christ the first person I talked to when I was thankful or had good news, the first I consulted when I was angry or upset, and the one I went to for strength and support. This represents a huge conversion in my journey from cradle to Catholic.

If there was a how-to book for becoming a friend, it would include the following step: spend time with the friend listening to them, sharing with them, and getting to know them. This is what prayer is.

Prayer is establishing a relationship with Christ through conversation, a conversation that includes both listening and talking. You cannot fully have a relationship with someone you do not spend time with; you must feed the relationship. The more you feed your relationship with Christ, the more He becomes a part of your life. Prayer, especially our most perfect form of public prayer, the Mass, is the place we nourish our relationship with Christ. It is this nurturing of the relationship with Jesus that makes our faith strong or makes our faith *grow*. We must spend our lifetime building this relationship, so we can reap the benefits during times of need or upon final judgment.

Recall your first real boyfriend or girlfriend. Typically, when you first met, you probably talked on the phone for hours and hours. (In today's language, I suppose you would text message, e-mail, or instant message for hours and hours.) You longed to be with this person every free moment, and you counted the minutes until your next meeting or waited by the phone for the next phone call. Believe it or not, the same holds true with our relationship with God. God is sitting around waiting for your call. He longs to spend time with you. When we neglect our friends or a boyfriend/girlfriend, it causes the relationship to suffer. The same is true in our relationship with God; however, unlike human relationships, God will never abandon you. Ever.

---

"Have no anxiety at all, but in everything, by prayer and petition, with thanksgiving, make your requests known to God. Then the peace of God that surpasses all understanding will guard your hearts and minds in Christ Jesus" (Phil. 4:6–7).

# 13
# The Eleventh Step

Alcoholics Anonymous (AA) has a twelve-step program as part of their recovery process. The eleventh step includes turning control over to a higher power through prayer and meditation. As Catholics, our higher power is the one true God. We state it in our creed each Sunday, "We believe in one God, the Father Almighty, maker of heaven and earth."

A few years ago, I heard a wonderful presentation given by a recovering addict who told of his recovery from drugs and alcohol. When he arrived at the step where he was to pray, he was lost. Like myself, he had been Catholic his whole life, but when it came time to pray, he realized he didn't know how. His prayer simply became, "Help me." That was it, two simple words. Yes, this is prayer. This is conversation with God. Today, this gentleman is very prayerful and knows how to pray, but it took a lot of practice.

I'll always remember my first days as the director of religious education. I wanted to lead prayer with confidence and was out to prove to Catholics that spontaneous prayer is not so intimidating. The reality for me up until this time, however, was that I also listened in awe as people like my son's non-Catholic Boy Scout troop leaders led prayers for the troop. When asked by the troop leaders to lead a meal prayer on one campout, I panicked at my potential inadequacy and recited the rote before-meal prayer all Catholics know, "Bless us, O Lord, and these thy gifts which we are about to receive, from thy bounty, through Christ our Lord. Amen." However, in my new role, I knew I would be expected to lead prayer. In those first days, I would go home and compose some very nice prayers, memorize them, and then recite them later as if they were spontaneous. I call these my fake spontaneous prayers. It seems comical to recall these prayers in retrospect, but that was what I felt I needed to do in order to feel successful at spontaneous prayer. The good news is that the more prayers I wrote, the easier it became to actually speak spontaneously in conversation with God.

The lesson for me was to practice prayer. Today, I no longer prewrite my spontaneous prayers. I have practiced it so much that I prefer the real spontaneous prayer because it comes from the heart. At the same time, I will always recognize my need for the rote prayers in my life. Either way, I practice them both. I tell my students they cannot become better basketball players by watching the NBA on television. They are required to actively dribble, shoot, rebound, and run to become better at basketball. It takes practice. So many of our children today are willing to spend many hours practicing a sport, but so little time, if any, practicing prayer. Do the math in your family and determine how much time each day you spend driving to and from and practicing or watching/playing sports or doing other activities, and see if you can find just five minutes for prayer.

A second lesson for me on prayer came from a nurse who was teaching childbirth classes. When I was pregnant with my first child, the nurse explained there is a certain amount of space in our brains reserved for emotions. She went further to say if three-fourths of that space is taken up by pain, then that only leaves one-fourth of that area open to pleasure. Therefore, if we can fill that "emotion area" with relaxation, there is less room for pain to enter. This is the methodology behind the breathing exercises used in childbirth. Having given birth to three children, I can give evidence to this fact. When I focused on the pain, the labor pains were more intense; when I focused on my breathing, the pain seemed very minimal.

I will argue the same is true with prayer. The more we pray, the more we fill our hearts with Jesus's love. The more that space is filled with Jesus's love, the less room there is for hate. I remember confessing to a priest that I had spoken very unkindly to a difficult person in a phone conversation, and I was trying to do better. I told the priest I had prayed before the conversation, and he simply said in reply, "Imagine how bad the conversation would have been if you hadn't prayed first." I know he was right.

The following Native American folk story explains it a bit differently. An elder Cherokee was teaching his grandchildren about life. He said to them, "A fight is going on inside me. It is a terrible fight, and it is between two wolves. One wolf represents fear, anger, envy, sorrow, regret, greed, arrogance, self-pity, guilt, resentment, inferiority, lies, pride, and superiority. The other wolf stands for joy, peace, love, hope, sharing, serenity, humility, kindness, benevolence, friendship, empathy, generosity, truth, compassion, and faith. This same fight is going on inside of you and every other person too."

The children thought about it for a minute, and then one child asked his grandfather, "Which wolf will win?"

The old Cherokee simply replied, "The one I feed."

If I had a twelve-step program for learning to pray, there is no doubt I would challenge everyone to start every prayer with a prayer of thanks. Start prayer by focusing on your blessings. Even if the only blessing you can muster up is that you woke up for the day, pray in gratitude. Having an attitude of gratitude can change your whole outlook for the day. It is always my first step, and I challenge you to think of a better place to start than to thank God for all the gifts he has given you.

Feed your spirituality with prayer and reap the benefits of a true relationship with Christ. Public or private, spontaneous or rote, however you chose to pray, just do it. As the first and primary teachers of faith, parents must take the important step of teaching by modeling prayer. Parents should understand the importance of praying *with* their children, while never underestimating the power of praying *for* their children each day too.

According to the story of St. Monica, she prayed for the conversion of her womanizing, troublemaking son (who went on in life to become a great doctor of our church, St. Augustine), because her bishop once told her, "If you talked to God about your son as much as you talked to your son about God, you would get much further." I felt blessed to know this story of a loving mother patiently praying for her son when my son quit going to church for a period in his life. I prayed *for* him to God and sometimes through St. Monica many, many nights. Whether or not it contributed to his return to the church, I felt like I was doing something more productive than lecturing him. He certainly received the occasional nudge or reminder because it is my baptismal call, and as a bonus, I received much comfort from praying.

The most common question I am asked at presentations is, "What do I do for my child who has left the church?" My answer is always to pray like St. Monica.

---

"Most important of all, pray to God to set your feet in the path of truth" (Sir. 37:15).

# 14
# Father, Son, and Holy Syrup

Today, I might pray on my drive to work, while mowing the lawn, in a peaceful adoration chapel, in the shower, or in my classroom before students arrive. I might pray several times a day or only once. I might pray for a brief second, a few minutes, or a whole hour. I just begin by talking to God, Jesus, the Holy Spirit, Mary, or the saints as if they were sitting next to me. Sometimes I pray out loud, sometimes in the quiet of my heart. I don't worry about using "holy words," I just speak. I am not an expert on prayer. The truth is there is no such thing as a prayer expert, but if you need some expert advice, watch children pray.

When my youngest daughter was first learning to pray, she used to start with the words, "Father, Son, and Holy Syrup." I am confident she didn't know she was praying the doxology at the time, but what is important was her heart, and she was praying with all of it. Children don't care too much about holy words or rules when they pray. They don't try to impress anyone; they just speak what's on their minds.

Pope John Paul II once wrote, "What enormous power the prayer of children has! This becomes a model for grown-ups themselves: praying with simple and complete trust means praying as children pray." I cannot count the number of times children have been a powerful witness to me through their conversations with God.

For example, the first time I was trying to teach my youngest about the prayer called the Rosary, she informed me that she knew what it was so I let her show me. She grabbed a Rosary bead and said, "Dear

God, who's up in heaven, I can't wait to see you." Then she moved to the next bead saying, "Dear God, who's up in heaven, I love you." And she continued, bead after bead, "Dear God …"

Did she pray the Rosary right? I say, "Yes!"

The following examples from children help to teach some lessons everyone should know about prayer. They might even give an accurate representation of what God had in mind for His prayer time with you.

> Dear God,
> I think about you sometimes even when I'm not praying.
> Love, Elliott

Lesson: Sometimes praying is just listening or thinking about God. We mustn't always talk. The catechism calls prayer, "the raising of one's mind and heart to God" (CCC 2259).

> God, Thank you for my baby brother, but what I prayed for was a puppy. Joyce.

Lesson: God does always answer our prayers. In the Gospel of Matthew, we are told, "Ask and it will be given to you; seek and you will find; knock and the door will be opened to you" (Matt. 7:7). Maybe we don't get the answer *we* want, but He constantly gives us the answer we *need*. Sometimes we are fortunate enough to know why God answered the way He did, but not always. We must trust He knows best.

"Do not be troubled if you do not immediately receive from God what you ask him; for he desires to do something even greater for you, while you cling to him in prayer" (CCC 2737).

> Dear God, If you watch in church on Sunday, I will show you my new shoes. Mickey D.

Lesson: At minimum, let us never forget God is always at church, but more important, He is also *always* with us outside of the building church. He dwells within us. Secondly, He already knows about your new shoes, but He still longs for you to tell Him about them. Prayer is about relationship.

Dear God,
I bet it is very hard for you to love all of everybody in the whole world. There are only four people in our family and I can never do it. Nan

Lesson: Even when it's hard, prayer allows us to love everyone, even our enemies. This is the example Christ left us. He says,

> And if you do good to those who do good to you, what credit is that to you? Even sinners do the same. If you lend money to those from whom you expect repayment, what credit [is] that to you? Even sinners lend to sinners, and get back the same amount. But rather, love your enemies and do good to them and lend expecting nothing back; then your reward will be great and you will be children of the Most High, for he himself is kind to the ungrateful and the wicked. (Luke 6:33–36)

---

"Out of the mouths of babes and infants you have drawn a defense against your foes to silence enemy and avenger" (Ps. 8:3).

# Part IV
# Celebrate

*Become a Full, Active Participant
in the Sacraments*

◊

# 15
# Can I Get a Witness?

My personal prayer life today is very mature; however, my prayer journey began with the very public prayer called the Mass. Because I was starting over on my faith journey, I began by praying this prayer first. I simply returned to the Mass I had left in college because it was all I knew to do. I started by going through the motions, and then I became a participant. Although participating fully in the Mass has provided me with the most growth, I am amazed at how God reached me the times I was present in body more than I was present in mind and heart. By simply being in the practice of attending Sunday Mass, I was moving my faith to the front of my consciousness for at least one hour each week.

When I was growing up, my family was very private about their faith. I don't ever recall sitting around the table discussing faith or having my parents tell me to share Christ with my neighborhood friends. It seemed we were very good at being Catholics in private, but the words *witness* or *evangelize* appeared to be four-letter words in our Catholic home.

Fortunately, one does not have to stand on a street corner preaching to passersby from a pulpit to give a witness to his or her faith. St. Francis of Assisi says, "Preach the Gospel at all times, and if necessary use words." A witness does not have to know all the answers or be a living saint. Being a witness can be as simple as attending the Sunday Eucharist.

My father made sure we *never*—I mean *never*—missed Sunday Mass. Through his commitment, I somehow knew faith was something *huge*; it was *very important* to my father. So sometimes, being a witness is just setting the tone like my father did for me. Like my father, I set the tone in my own house, and we *never* missed Mass.

The very first place for you to witness is within your own family by praying together and celebrating the Eucharist on Sundays and holy days of obligation. Attending Mass allows you to make a statement about the importance of faith in your life and should be the foundation for all Catholics. It was the first place I started on my journey back, and it is where the apostles started after Christ's death. "Every day they devoted themselves to meeting together in the temple area and to breaking bread in their homes" (Acts 2:46).

Thank goodness these first followers of Christ were committed to celebrating this meal, and thank goodness they witnessed through this gathering and set an example for us to share in the Eucharist we have today. Like the apostles, we must confidently go out and witness. In Acts 2:40, we see the results of such a witness by Peter: "He testified with many other arguments, and was exhorting them, 'Save yourselves from this corrupt generation.' Those who accepted his message were baptized, and about three thousand persons were added that day."

Every time you gather for Mass, even when it's hard for you to be there or your heart and mind are not quite committed to it, it is an opportunity to witness. It is also an opportunity to encounter Christ and receive his grace. Imagine if you showed up for Mass and no one else was present in the pews. What message does that empty church send? Most likely, it says, "This sacrament Jesus left for His people is not important." On the other hand, a full church tells us, "This encounter with Christ through this sacrament of sacrifice and meal is important to the life of everyone gathered."

Our family sits in the front pews at church. It is somewhat necessary because I can't see or hear very well. It is also a very conscious decision I have made as a relentless Catholic mother. When I was growing up, my family always sat in the last pew, and I was easily distracted and unable to really experience what was going on. My children sat in the front pews because I wanted them to be able to see the important events taking place. I know it was not their preference, but they knew enough not to sit in the back. Over the years, people from our church that we did not know would recognize us when we were out in the community. This confused my husband and me a bit, until these people started to share stories with us about the memories they have of our children growing up in front of them in the pews at church. We couldn't see them, but they were able to observe us each week. My husband was recently told by someone who sat in the pews behind us how much they used to enjoy watching him handle our youngest daughter at Mass on Sundays. One family shared that they used to take bets on how long it would be before she would throw her shoes off, and another said how much patience and love they witnessed through watching my husband dealing with her adventures. Now that's a witness.

In reflecting on this now, I realize that I also have spent many hours in the pews looking at those around me and letting them witness to me. I have seen a young couple very busy with three small children, and yet they are all impeccably dressed in suits for the boys and dresses, stockings, and hair bows for the girls, and I am impressed by their commitment. I have seen an adult child bringing a feeble mother to Mass each Sunday. I have seen a couple bringing their very handicapped, noncommunicative son to Mass every week, showing great compassion and love. I have seen beautiful singers sharing their gift with an entire community by leading songs and young altar servers showing respect to the altar. I have seen couples sharing an embrace at the sign of peace and a priest who has devoted his life and sacrificed for the purpose of spreading God's Kingdom and saving souls. Each of these persons has been a witness to me just by being present. I know I am a better person having witnessed them at Mass, and I feel blessed to have developed relationships with many of them.

Since returning to the sacrament of Eucharist over twenty years ago, I have remained faithful to my commitment to this prayer in my life. Not only have I learned it is something I need for my spiritual nourishment, I have also learned the value of just being there. In retrospect, I know it was simply my presence at Mass in my youth that guided me back to the Eucharist. If you have removed this sacrament from your life, I challenge you to return and become a witness.

---

"I give thanks to my God at every remembrance of you, praying always with joy in my every prayer for all of you, because of your partnership for the gospel from the first day until now" (Phil. 1:4).

# 16
# Let Me Entertain You

I admit I have said, "Mass is boring." I've said it many times in my life, and I am not proud to admit it. Each time I ask a group if they have spoken similar words, the majority—if not all—will admit to expressing this sentiment at one time in their lives. Perhaps you too have found yourself thinking or speaking the same. Our world is inundated with constant media messages designed to entertain and empower. As a result, many have come to expect a society that caters to their wants. Unfortunately, some have this expectation for their faith experiences too. They want to be wowed by hip music and moved by theatrical sermons.

There is no doubt our Catholic faith is countercultural to our world today. All one has to do is watch a few television commercials to become aware of the priorities of our society. The secular crowd says, "Do what makes you happy," while Jesus tells us to be humble. Our world tells us to execute criminals; Jesus tells us to forgive. Businesses say, "Buy this," Jesus tells us to give. The world says, "Do what feels good." Jesus says, "Sometimes love hurts." Many in our nation accept abortion, cloning, and euthanasia, while the Word of God asks us to respect the dignity of all life because it is a gift from God.

In a world where the antics of Hollywood stars adorn most magazine covers, we are reminded that secular messages often speak louder than the message of the Bible and Christ. Part of that message has our children believing they shouldn't have to go to Mass because it is boring. Having fun or being entertained with our faith is not a bad concept in and of itself; however, we should always be prepared to take faith experiences at face value, entertaining or not. If Mass is boring for you, I would argue you are not trying hard enough. Once I moved from being an observer at Mass to being a participant, I discovered Mass to be anything but boring.

When I started to lector for my parish, part of my preparation meant thoroughly examining each reading in order to better proclaim it. I recall trying to prepare for a difficult reading from the letter of St. Paul one weekend. At first glance, and after my first few practices, the reading seemed to be a group of random clauses that didn't go together. I was having trouble getting it clear, so I kept repeating it until about the tenth time when the proverbial lightbulb went off. I wish I could recall the reading, but suffice it to say, Paul's words spoke to me in a very powerful way. Though I can't recall the words, I can certainly recall how I felt when I heard God speak directly to me through this reading. It was both comforting and powerful. So today, I actively seek that feeling through the readings at every Mass whether I am a lector or not.

As a participant at Mass, I have drawn deeper into the Liturgy of the Word, which has been nothing short of *entertaining*. Each time I celebrate the Eucharist, I pray for help to hear what I need to hear in the readings or the homily, and I am amazed at how many times God seems to be speaking directly to me. Now that's *never* boring. When I realized my priest is acting in the person of Christ as he recalls the Last Supper, I was inspired, not bored. And when I discovered Christ is truly present, I was motivated to go to Mass more often. When I was an observer at Mass, the readings were often those random clauses rolling over the top of my head. Knowing what I know now about putting effort into hearing God's Word, I don't ever want to miss the opportunity to hear what He has to say to me because I wasn't paying attention or trying hard enough.

Being a witness at Mass includes being a *participant*. The *General Instruction of the Roman Missal* (*GIRM*) calls for "full, active, and conscious participation" in the Mass. Being a participant means listening prayerfully to the Word of God in the readings; praising and worshiping God through the singing of songs and the reciting of prayers and Psalms; offering thanksgiving, petitions, and gifts to God;

becoming living tabernacles through the reception of the Body and Blood of Christ; and opening our hearts to leave Mass to go and love and serve the Lord in our world today.

If you truly come to Eucharist with the understanding that you are a participant, each Mass is entertaining in the fulfilling sense of the word. Stop for a moment and imagine you are participating in the Last Supper with Christ. In your imagination, picture yourself sitting alongside the other disciples in Leonardo da Vinci's painting, *The Last Supper*. Do you imagine yourself being bored as you listen to Christ and break bread with Him? If not, recognize this scene as the gift of Eucharist, not as a boring ritual.

There are countless ways to be entertained in our world today. When one attends a professional basketball game or visits a movie theater, he or she sits in a seat and is entertained. Entertainment is the purpose of these venues. This is not the purpose of the Eucharist. Entertainment is optional; participation is not.

I know my students often expect to be entertained by my lessons. I remind them the goal of attending school is to learn; if they are entertained in the process, that is a bonus. The same goes for Mass. The goal is to have an encounter with Christ, to receive His grace and nourish your faith. Entertaining or not, this far surpasses the rewards I get from an exciting basketball game or an entertaining movie. When I have looked at the preparation and reception of the sacraments as an obligation or something I have to do, I can admit I have left disappointed. However, when I look at the preparation and reception of each of the sacraments as an opportunity to encounter Christ, I am never disappointed.

If you find yourself making excuses for attending mass, it could be because you are looking to be entertained. If you're looking to be entertained, you are attending as an observer. If you find yourself not understanding the Mass, I pray the following two chapters will help you. Until then, just go to mass. Start by taking your body there, and God will take care of your mind and heart to change you to a participant. He's that good. At a minimum, the action of attending mass needs to become a part of your habits. There is a quote I share with my students. The author is unknown, but I believe it is inspired by God and sums up my message.

Watch your thoughts, they become your words.

Watch your words, they become your actions.
Watch your actions, they become your habits.
Watch your habits, they become your character.
Watch your character, it becomes your destiny.

---

"Give thanks to the Lord, invoke his name; make known among the nations his deeds. Sing to him, sing his praise, proclaim all his wondrous deeds. Glory in his holy name; rejoice, O hearts that seek the Lord! Look to the Lord in his strength; seek to serve him constantly" (1 Chron. 16:8–11).

# 17
# May the Force Be with You

A common response I receive from parents in my work is, "I can't force my children to go to church or participate in the sacraments." There was even a time in my life when I was persuaded or inclined to agree with this sentiment. Perhaps you have caught yourself thinking the same thing. This comment reminds me of a time in my life when I felt forced to go to church by my parents. In retrospect, I recognize this time as the period in my life I did not see the value in this sacrament or appreciate the gift that it truly was. This leads me to believe this is the same reason parents feel they would have to force a child to be with Christ in the Eucharist.

When told by parents, "I can't force my children to go to church," my first reply is always, "Why not?" (refer to chapter 3: "Who's the Boss?"). My second response can be shared through one of the many stories in the Bible in which people recognized Christ as the Messiah and did anything within their power just to be near him and touch his cloak (see Matt. 9:20–22, Mark 6:53–56, Mark 2:1–12, and John 6:1–2) or the apostles who left their livelihoods behind to follow Jesus (see Mark 1:20). These people understood the value of meeting Jesus and following him. From these stories, it is clear that no one forced these people to want to be in the presence of Jesus.

The issue isn't that we force children to participate in the sacraments; it is that we are neglecting to show them the value of being with Christ. An encounter with Christ is exactly what each of the sacraments offers us. In effect, children are really telling parents, "You are not showing me how this is relevant in my life."

I have never had a parent ask me, "What do I tell my child if he asks me why I force him to go to school?" It seems parents are equipped to respond to this question by showing the value of learning. Shouldn't the same be true with our faith?

All of my children go to school. I see learning as a privilege; they see it as a burden. Yet, I *force* them to go because I know it will help them learn and grow. As you recall from earlier chapters, I get to make this decision as the parent. I *force* them to go to doctors and dentists, too. My children certainly do not always enjoy going to these places, but I doubt anyone would think I was a bad parent for forcing them to go. Keeping children from church and the sacraments denies them an opportunity to experience Christ as He desired. Furthermore, it sends the message that these sacraments are not important. My husband considers the time I forced him to come to adoration with me and the time I forced him to go on a retreat to be the two most important events in his faith journey. He says I forced him because I simply signed him up and told him when to arrive; I say I provided him an opportunity to grow. We were both right.

I would argue further that the idea children are *forced* to celebrate Mass denies the fact that Mass is a celebration. Ask yourself how many children would say to their parents, "Do I *have* to go to the birthday party?" I would venture to guess few, if any, children would protest having to participate in this celebration. If a comparison between a birthday party and the Eucharistic celebration seems unreasonable to you, consider the following:

> Birthday parties gather families and friends together; so does the Mass.
> We sing at birthday parties; we sing at Mass.
> We bring gifts to both celebrations, we eat at both celebrations, and we give thanks at both celebrations.
> We light birthday candles to demonstrate the presence of each year of life. We light candles at Mass to demonstrate the presence of Christ.
> We share stories at birthday parties, and we share stories through scripture at Mass.

Although birthday parties typically last longer than an hour, the similarities certainly indicate both events are truly celebrations. If children understand Eucharist is a celebration, perhaps they won't feel forced to go or have the desire to ask why they *have* to go.

Recall Mark Twain's character Tom Sawyer who gets his friends to paint a picket fence for him by bragging about how much fun it was. In a similar fashion, when my eldest daughter was five years old, I could force her to bring me a box from across a room by saying, "Oh, I was going to have you bring me that box, but I bet it is too heavy for you to lift. I guess I can see if your big brother is strong enough to carry it to me." Invariably, in her desire to please her mother and make me proud, she would bring me the box. It would not have sounded as fun if I simply said, "Go get that box for me." When I gave her the opportunity to show me how strong or grown up she was, she became a willing participant.

Tom Sawyer does not force his friends to paint; nor did I force my daughter to deliver a box to me. The difference is the value received from participating in these activities. The value in painting Tom Sawyer's fence was fun and friendship. The value in bringing her mother a box was appreciation or kindness. There is a faith lesson in this reverse psychology. When we show children the value of attending the celebration of the Mass, they become more willing to be participants. The value of attending Mass is an encounter with Christ. Children are forced to go to church when they're too little to understand it, but parents bring these young children in order to share with them the joy they receive from this celebration. The parents see the value, and they are doing these children a favor by passing on and sharing the faith.

When I decided I was ready to grow as a Catholic, I returned to the Mass I was forced to attend as a child. I knew Mass was important to my family, so I believed it had value. In fact, it was instrumental in bringing me back to my faith. It was perhaps the most important step I took on my journey from cradle to Catholic. When part of my life felt empty, I forced myself to attend Mass, and I have since received much joy and peace from this celebration. I searched for the value in going to Mass. I came to believe Christ is truly present at Mass, and then nothing could force me to stay away.

In the George Lucas Star Wars films, references are made to "the

Force." In these films, the *force* means the goodness or the opposite of the dark side. I have often felt the Star Wars "Force" was a very spiritual idea. Scripture tells us when we sin, we are walking in the darkness, and to avoid darkness (or the dark side), we should walk in the light of Christ by following Him (see John 8:12). In Star Wars, the Force is a very positive thing; however, in faith, the word *force* is often used negatively to keep Catholics from faith. I appreciate Mr. Lucas associating the word *force* with goodness, and I believe the same can be done with our faith. Although the word *force* does have a negative meaning outside of Star Wars or physics, it hardly seems negative to say you force your children to experience Christ.

If a child inquires about being forced to go to church and you struggle to show them the value of the Mass, I would suggest you haven't found the value yourself. If so, go find it as I did by going back and participating fully. In the meantime, if a child questions, "Why are you forcing me to go to church?" simply reply, "I love you so much I want to give you every opportunity to see God's love for you." If necessary, remind them you are the boss and that the Bible supports you with the scripture at the end of this chapter. "May the force be with you."

---

"Remember to keep holy the Sabbath day. Six days you may labor and do all your work, but the seventh day is the Sabbath of the Lord your God … Honor your father and your mother" (Exod. 20:8–9, 12).

# 18
# Catholic Calisthenics

There are things all of us do in life without much thought, like breathing. The mindless act of breathing demonstrates that it's sometimes okay to just go through the motions because it keeps you practicing—or maybe even alive. In faith, I have found many things I did without thinking were useful to have stored in my memory. My story of the Rosary was a clear example of this. I went through the motions of saying this prayer enough that it was there in that desperate hour when I needed it.

Catholics kneel in church, and then we sit, and then we stand. And then we sit again, stand again, sit, stand, bow, kneel, stand, shake hands, kneel, stand, kneel, sit, stand, genuflect, stand, etc. It's what I call Catholic calisthenics. Sometimes these gestures seem tedious, but when meaning is assigned to them, they are more than just exercises. Sometimes it is just a start.

Recently, a discussion came up at a Catholic school about the disrespectful manner in which the students were genuflecting. It was decided teachers would direct students to genuflect in a reverent manner and correct those not doing so. I argued that when the students understood *why* they needed to genuflect, they would *want* to genuflect.

I have always genuflected when I enter my pew at Mass. My parents told me to do it, so I would go through the motions as a child without even thinking about it. I now know that genuflecting toward the tabernacle with reverence as I enter my pew says, "I understand I am in the presence of Christ; I'm in awe of it, and it's worthy of my knee touching the ground before it." Imagine if you actually saw Christ present in the flesh standing before that tabernacle. Would you not prostrate yourself to the ground before it? In history, we genuflected before kings as a sign of respect. Today, we stand at attention when the president of the United States enters a room as a sign of respect. Our Lord and Savior deserves similar displays of respect and signs of reverence. We need to give children an appreciation of why we do what we do at Mass. Research shows children want their faith to be relevant. Even in education, when students find the information being taught relevant to their lives, they are more willing learners. If we assign meaning, the benefits are powerful.

We stand during the Gospel reading to demonstrate we are at full attention, while we sit to show we are sharing in a common meal and to show we are ready to receive God's message in the readings. We bow our heads at certain points in the Mass to show respect.

From the words and actions to the hymns, I was amazed when I realized how much the Mass is rooted in scripture. Through the readings alone, if one was to attend daily Mass for three years, one would have heard almost the entire Bible proclaimed to them. This is an easy way to "read" the entire Bible. As a way of helping me move from simply doing Catholic calisthenics to being a witness at Mass, I assigned meaning to the things I used to call boring and meaningless by discovering them in scripture. Below is a list of my top fifteen findings. Take a moment to look up these passages and assign meaning to this beautiful gift Christ has left for you. I pray it draws you closer to the Eucharist as it did me. Once you are through, you may better be able to educate your children on the importance of the actions seen at this celebration.

1) Christ asks us to remember the Sabbath in his memory (Deut. 5:12–16, 1 Cor. 11:23–31, John 6:47–58).
2) The disciples followed the example Jesus left for them at the Last Supper and passed it down until this Passover meal became the Eucharist we celebrate today (Acts 2:42–46).
3) Christ is present in the gathering of the people (Matt. 18:20).
4) We sing in thanksgiving and praise (Psalms 9, 33, 95, 98, 106).

5) We sing the Gloria (Luke 2:14).
6) Christ is present in the readings (1 Thess. 2:13).
7) We offer petitions (1 Tim. 2:1–3).
8) We sing Hosanna in the Highest (Matt. 21:6–9).
9) The Last Supper is recalled (Matt. 26, Mark 14, Luke 22).
10) We pray the Our Father (Matt. 6:5–13).
11) We offer the sign of peace/penitence (Matt. 5:23–24).
12) We say the Lamb of God (John 1:29).
13) Christ is revealed in the breaking of the bread (Luke 24:13–35).
14) Christ gives us all we need in the bread (Luke 9:16–17).
15) We offer repentance prior to Communion (Luke 7:6–7).

---

"On the night he was handed over, he took bread, and, after he had given thanks, broke it and said, 'This is my body that is for you. Do this in remembrance of me.' In the same way also the cup, after supper, saying, 'This cup is the new covenant in my blood. Do this as often as you drink it, in remembrance of me.' For as often as you eat this bread and drink the cup, you proclaim the death of the Lord until he comes" (1 Cor. 11:23–31).

# 19
# Casual Sundays

It was a lazy, cold, winter Sunday in December, and I opted to wear jeans to Mass, something I very rarely do. Even though I am most comfortable in sweatpants and an oversized sweatshirt most days, dressing up for Mass is a choice I make. Do I believe God will accept me at Mass "as is"? You bet! All one has to do is look at scripture to realize Jesus didn't preach in fancy clothes. One can also learn through scripture that Jesus did not judge others by their appearances; he hung out with the marginalized, the lepers, the outcasts, etc. As the King of Kings, he was a humble man, even in dress.

So, this particular Sunday, I chose to wear jeans, which my two daughters picked up right away. "Can we wear jeans?" they asked with some cynicism. Knowing I could never ask them to do more than I was willing to do myself, I relented with some trepidation. As our family entered church, the ushers reminded us that it was our day to bring the gifts to the altar for offertory—a detail I had overlooked in the busy, lazy, cold December rush. As my seventeen-year-old daughter would tell the story, I was *devastated* we were going to bring up the gifts wearing jeans. I will confess, though not devastated, I was disappointed. I thought to myself, "This is an opportunity for our family to be a witness to the importance of this ministry, and this is the best we can show them." Since failing to serve was a worse offense, we brought up the gifts anyway, with no fatalities.

Suffice it to say, I do not believe people who wear jeans to Mass are less holy than those who don't. I believe what is written in 1 Peter 3:3–4:

> Your adornment must not be merely external—braiding the hair, and wearing gold jewelry, or putting on dresses; but let it be the hidden person of the heart, with the imperishable quality of a gentle and quiet spirit, which is precious in the sight of God.

However, I ask you to consider the wedding tuxedo.

Most individuals do not think twice about renting a tuxedo for a wedding ceremony, and young men rent them for high-school dances. A potential bride dreams of the day she gets to don the glamorous gown for her wedding. Young women preparing for a high-school dance go to a beautician to get an "up-do," go to a manicurist to have their nails done, have a salon professionally do their makeup, and spend many dollars on a dress and shoes they will have on for a few hours. I know my family does not dress with this same type of fervor in preparing for Mass. However, even my small efforts to dress up for Mass, though they seem like a sacrifice on some days, are part of my job as a witness to the others who will be gathered.

People are very aware that dressing up takes more effort. When individuals make the extra effort to dress for a wedding or special occasion, they are recognizing the event as a special day. I would argue each Mass is a special event too. It is a time to *encounter* Christ, to hear God speak to us through the Word, and to receive Christ into our bodies through Communion. That seems pretty special to me. When my family is expecting company, we all tidy up our areas and clean the house for our guests. Imagine if Christ was to show up at your house this evening. Do you think you might clean up a bit? If so, why not clean up when you go to meet Him in the sacraments?

I debated with my oldest two children about what to wear for a job interview at a fast-food restaurant. I suggested they wear nice pants and a dress shirt. They thought jeans and a T-shirt would do. I won the battle, but the war is far from over. The reality of our world is that the term *dress up* has a new definition, and the phrase *Sunday best* is no longer part of our vernacular. All I need to do is go to the local mall and see how the employees are dressed. I am constantly amazed at what our secular world accepts in regards to clothing: underwear showing, pelvises exposed, and jeans showered with holes in inappropriate places. I am not writing to judge those who wear jeans to Mass. I do agree with the adage, "You can't judge a book by its cover"; however, I challenge you to adopt the habit of dressing up for Mass and for all the sacraments to enforce the attitude that these are important events. They are celebrations!

# 20
# Love Is Like a Rose

Staying close to the Eucharist was instrumental in my faith journey. Yet, God left us *seven* outward signs of His Grace through his Son called the sacraments. In his infinite wisdom, God knew we would need, like doubting Thomas, to see and touch His presence in our lives. This certainly would explain why He sent the Son in the flesh. The sacraments provide us with these opportunities through sacramentals. For example, the water poured over an infant at baptism is a sacramental that provides us with something we can see and touch to remind us of God's great love for us.

To put it another way, consider the following. A wife may know her husband loves her, just like we could all confidently say God loves us. Her husband might even tell her he loves her in his words, just like God tells us of His love through the Bible. Finally, her husband might show her his love by sending her a dozen roses. Although she is aware of her husband's love, it is nice—and sometimes necessary—to receive an outward sign of love that can be seen and touched. The same is true for the sacraments. How brilliant is our heavenly Father to know we would need these physical reminders showered upon us at different times in our lives.

I realized I had to celebrate all the sacraments to continue growing in my faith. I had already come back to the Eucharist but was a bit reluctant to return to the sacrament of reconciliation. Being away from this outward sign of God's love for me made it harder for me to celebrate forgiveness in my life. There were things I needed to be forgiven for, and there were people I needed to forgive. It was hard to celebrate the sacrament of reconciliation, because I was not celebrating reconciliation in my own life. Conversely, it was hard to celebrate reconciliation in my life, because I was not celebrating it in the sacrament. It reminds me of the old question, "What came first, the chicken or the egg?" For me, I had to bring the sacrament back into my life in order to share it with others.

In the parable of the unforgiving servant, a servant who is forgiven his large debt later refuses to forgive the small debt of a fellow servant. The unforgiving servant is handed over to the torturers by his master and told, "So will my heavenly Father do to you, unless each of you forgives his brother from his heart" (Matt. 18:35). The servant was offered forgiveness very freely just as Christ offers it to each of us. However, Christ is also telling us in this parable to offer forgiveness in the same way to those who have offended us. In the Gospel of Luke, He says, "And if you need to offer forgiveness to those in your life, do as Christ tells his disciples, 'If [your brother] wrongs you seven times in a day and returns to you seven times saying, 'I am sorry,' you should forgive him" (Luke 17:4). By neglecting the sacrament of reconciliation, I was not accepting the forgiveness Christ's death on the cross made available to me. Once I became willing to accept this forgiveness for myself, I had to recognize that Christ's death was for forgiveness of all sins, not just mine. In other words, I had to be willing to share that same forgiveness.

In 2007, I conducted an informal survey of Catholic school parents whose children were preparing for the sacrament of reconciliation. It showed that 44 percent believed they did not need to confess to a priest. Furthermore, the average time since the parents' last confession was 5.5 years. This data is a bit scary when one realizes these parents are the primary teachers of faith for these children. We have already learned the data tells us children look to parents in making faith decisions. If parents are not modeling reconciliation within the family setting by letting the children see parents apologize and offer forgiveness to each other or by participating in the sacrament, then children will not appreciate the value or reap the benefits of reconciliation.

Sacraments are part of every Catholic's spiritual journey. They are all found in scripture through the story of Jesus's life. Each one has meaning and relevance, and each is a sign of God's love. Even when it feels rote, trust that Christ knew what He was doing when He left these gifts for us and celebrate anyway. If you are present and celebrating with an open heart, He will take care of the rest. Every time you celebrate the sacraments, it gives you a chance to be a witness; it is an opportunity for the Spirit to work in your life, and it is a chance for you to be with Christ and receive His Grace.

My youngest daughter recently celebrated her first reconciliation two days before Thanksgiving. On the drive home, she declared, "I'm going to try and make it to Thanksgiving without sinning."

When my oldest daughter completed her first reconciliation, our priest was trying to remind her that she would need the sacrament more than once in her life. He asked her if she might sin again. "No," she insisted. Three times he asked her, rephrasing it so as to help her understand that we all sin even if we are trying not to sin. All three times, she emphatically replied, "I will never sin again, Father." It is comical to share these stories, but in reality, sin and our need for reconciliation is a real challenge in our lives. The important lesson in these stories is that the sacrament left my daughters feeling so good about themselves—so loved—they wanted to do their best to keep that feeling. That is what all sacraments should do for us. If you don't agree, I would argue again you are not trying hard enough. How could you not feel good getting a "dozen roses" from God?

When I was growing up, I remember being very afraid and anxious about the sacrament of reconciliation. I remember feeling like the priest sitting on the other side of that sliding screen was judging me by my sins. I admit it was not the happiest of memories. I used to present the same list of sins for most of my confessions in my school days. I always disobeyed my parents and fought with my brother and sisters or cheated at board games. Occasionally, I would confess to stealing a pencil from someone at school (whether I really did or not) because I thought it sounded like a small, forgivable infraction of the seventh commandment and it gave me some variety.

Today, I don't fear the confessional room. I visit my priest face-to-face, and I am filled with so much peace that I want to go back. My confessions today do not include a list; they include conversation about the struggles and challenges I am facing in being a follower of Christ, and I am given counsel and encouragement. I recognize it as the gift it truly is. By changing my outlook and my approach to this beautiful sacrament, I am able to experience the same feelings my daughters felt on their first reconciliation.

If it has been a while since your last confession, find your way back like the prodigal son (Luke 15:11–32). Just as in this parable, you will be greeted with open arms. If you have had a bad experience with the sacrament, tell your confessor. If you have forgotten how to receive the sacrament, ask your confessor to help you. If you are scared, pray for the courage to receive. If you have anything weighing heavy on your heart, give God the chance to forgive you through the sacrament. After all, that is the very reason he died for us. Finally, if you think it is enough to tell your sins to God, consider the following example.

If I am a piano player in a band who continually misses all my notes during concert performances because of poor effort on my part, I have offended many people. I have offended the band members who count on me to hit the proper notes. I have offended the concertgoers who paid for a quality performance, and perhaps I have offended the song's composer or pianists everywhere. Is it enough to tell God I am sorry for playing poorly, or do I need to seek forgiveness from the larger group? In this example, the poor actions were not just between the pianist and God; they obviously affected many more. In the last chapter, I spoke about how my family was unaware that we were witnesses simply by our presence at Mass. In the same way, we are unaware of how many are truly affected by our sins. A sin is an offense against all Christians no matter who witnesses it. To reconcile means to bring back together. Reconciliation welcomes us back into our Christian community and helps us grow the Kingdom of God. Now that's something to celebrate!

---

"I tell you, in just the same way there will be more joy in heaven over one sinner who repents than over ninety-nine righteous people who have no need of repentance" (Luke 15:7).

# Part V
# **Learn**

*Increase Your Knowledge of Your Faith*

☙

# 21
# An "F" in Religion

I was in high school and had gathered with some friends to play a game of Trivial Pursuit. I was the only Catholic playing, and I'll never forget one of the questions asked of me on that day over twenty-five years ago. The question was, "What are the letters over Christ's head on the crucifix?" All my friends protested about how unfair that question was—a shoo-in for any Catholic. My faced turned several shades of red as I failed to come up with the correct response. If you're curious or want to test yourself, the correct answer is INRI, which stands for "Jesus of Nazareth, King of Jews." There is no "J" in the Latin alphabet, so the letter "I" is used. I know I disappointed my friends on that day (although they were not sad to keep me from advancing in the game), but I also disappointed all those who called themselves Catholic in that moment. Imagine the testimony I gave to my friends in not knowing the answer to that question? This is a moment I'll never forget, especially after realizing several years later that the question was far from trivial, because those letters represent the charge against our sacrificial lamb. I needed to know the answer for my spiritual growth, not for the purposes of winning a board game and sparing myself embarrassment.

On my faith journey, I made prayer a real part of my life, fell in love with the Eucharist, returned to the sacrament of reconciliation, and began to *grow*. I made the commitment to grow Catholic children, which meant I had the responsibility of learning the Catholic faith myself. This was my next step toward growth. I made the decision to study Catholicism, and I was committed to studying everything I could find. As I continued to study, I discovered my faith grew by leaps and bounds. My spiritual growth was only made possible by my studying and praying. I could not grow as a Catholic by simply willing it to be. I had to learn.

I was becoming like a sponge, absorbing everything I could about the Catholic faith. If I was reading a book, it was a book that would teach me something new or answer a question I had about Catholicism. There was a point when my husband forced me to give him a non-religious book title for him to purchase for me. I love reading books and receiving them as gifts, and he wanted to buy me a book for Christmas. I decided I would request the popular book *Angela's Ashes* by Frank McCourt. I wasn't sure what the book was about, but it was talked about a lot and I believed it to be about an Irishman. I have some Irish heritage, and Ireland was also another interest of mine, so I thought this would be a good diversion. My husband purchased the book for me, and I was surprised to find that I learned things about Catholicism by reading this memoir, much to the chagrin of my husband. In the chapter titled, "Frank or Frances," I will talk about why this was one of the most important Catholic books I have read.

I have the privilege of teaching religion and the task of assigning students the grade they have earned in religion class. Each year, though I try to warn my students, more than the occasional student will get a "C" or a "D" on their grade card. Every year, I have more than one student who asks me, "How can you grade my faith? That is between me and God." I agree wholeheartedly, much to their surprise.

At this point, these students eagerly wait for me to erase the grade and give them the "A" they believe they deserve. Unfortunately, this does not happen. Instead, I remind the students I am not grading their faith; I am simply grading their religious knowledge. I explain that knowledge of their religion is necessary in order to grow in faith. I share with them how my own spiritual growth came as a result of my study and how I continue to study today. I no longer receive a classroom grade for my religious studies, but I am vastly aware my study of religion is an ongoing, lifelong process.

Although religious knowledge can be taught, faith must be modeled. These two must work together; one cannot advance without the other. I may have my students read from a book, listen to me share a faith story, complete a worksheet, or do a group project in religion class to help them learn this content area, but I must also show them, by my example, how to be a follower of Christ.

Look at our master teacher. Christ himself taught by telling parables and sharing God's Word and by His example. For example, in the Sermon on the Mount, Jesus teaches the crowd a lesson on how to live by presenting the beatitudes (Luke 6:20–26). Jesus's forgiveness of the sinful woman (Luke 7:36–50) teaches by example, and Jesus's parable of the sower (Luke 8:4–10) shares a story to which the people can relate as a way to share faith. These are the examples we are given of how to learn about faith, and all of these methods can and should be used in the home.

As I explained in the last section, the more I learned about the Mass, the more I came to appreciate it and benefit from it. Knowledge is a gift of the Holy Spirit, and peace and joy are fruits of that same Spirit. I discovered the more knowledge I had about my faith, the more joy I received from it. This is why I test my students on their faith and make them research and study it. Encourage your children to study their faith, and study alongside them. Look for ways through your diocese and church to study your faith. Attend a Bible study class; attend a parish mission or retreat; read Catholic books; or volunteer to serve on a parish committee.

---

"Can a blind person guide a blind person? Will not both fall into a pit? No disciple is superior to the teacher; but when full trained, every disciple will be like his teacher" (Luke 6:39–40).

"He was praying in a certain place, and when he had finished, one of the disciples said to him, 'Lord, teach us to pray just as John taught his disciples'" (Luke 11:1).

# 22
# Explain It to Me Like I'm a Four-Year-Old

When I began my study of Catholicism, I wondered where to begin. I hadn't saved all my religion assignments from elementary school. I couldn't just take a university class on how to understand Catholicism, and it would have been hard to just ask my parents or a priest to answer every question because I didn't even know what questions to ask. So I began by doing two things: I bought a children's Bible, not a grown-up one—remember I had the spiritual maturity of an eighth-grader at best—and I volunteered at my church to teach CCD. Here's why.

The quote, "Explain it to me like I am a four-year-old," comes from the 1993 movie *Philadelphia*. Actor Denzel Washington plays a lawyer named Joe Miller who uses these words while interviewing a witness during a court trial. The purpose of these words in the movie was to make the valid point that if what a witness says in court makes sense to a four-year-old, then there is certainly no room for confusion for the jury. These words struck me so much that I use them myself frequently. They especially come in handy when my teenage children are attempting to explain away some mischief. My child begins filling the gaps in his or her story with things that don't make any sense in the hope of confusing me so I overlook the mischief. When asking someone to explain something to you like you are a four-year-old, the idea is that they should keep it simple enough for anyone to understand the answer. These words also provide much assistance in learning about and teaching our faith.

As parents, we like to think we are mature adults. This idea misguides us to the adult section of the library or bookstore. However, I encourage you to start your education in your faith in the children's section. Humble yourself; go back and relearn things you think you already know. It is equally important to graduate to the adult section, but for now, trust from my experience the value of learning things at a four-year-old level. I learned much from teaching second-graders because they allowed me to see my faith more purely, more innocently, and in a fully trusting way. This is what Jesus refers to when he says, "Truly I say to you, unless you are converted and become like children, you will not enter the kingdom of heaven" (Matt. 18:3). Learning my faith from a second-grade level also allowed me to see my faith explained in words I could easily understand.

Armed with my children's Bible and my Catholic school education, I felt confident I at least had the faith of a seven-year-old. That was a good starting point, and that is where I began teaching (and learning) about my faith, as a second-grade CCD teacher. In my second-grade teacher's annotated edition of the religion text, I had two things: a book that explained my faith in a way seven-year-olds could understand and footnotes that included helpful hints and answer keys to the questions in the children's books. As a volunteer catechist, I also had access to the valuable resource of two sisters who supervised me. However, I did not realize how much I would learn from the seven-year-olds I taught. Nor did I realize how challenging their questions would be. For example, "Are Adam and Eve in heaven?" The growing I did in that first year is the reason I continue to teach religion classes and to grow every day. Quite verifiably, to teach is to learn; to learn is to grow.

Perhaps you feel teaching is not one of your gifts, much like joining the choir would not be a good idea for me. Although I probably shouldn't be in the choir, I *do* sing from the pews and participate in the Mass fully. Likewise, you do not have to be a formal teacher. The Catholic Church already recognizes parents as the first and primary teachers of the faith to their children. You have undoubtedly taught your child many things—how to eat, how to tie shoes, how to ride a bike. By default of becoming a parent, you *are* a teacher—a teacher of tying shoes, a teacher of faith. You do not have to teach a classroom of students, but you do have to teach *your* child(ren). Begin by learning yourself, and then "Go preach the Gospel" (1 Cor. 9:16), especially to your own children.

I began learning by arming myself with tools of faith. I bought a children's Bible, used a children's CCD teacher book, and obtained resources from my parish and Catholic Web sites. I did not go out immediately and buy the Catechism of the Catholic Church or any intense, adult books on theology. When I look back at the resources I started with, I see they are quite childish. Conversely, when I look at the resources that once intimidated me, I feel blessed to now understand them. I can recognize this as the gifts of wisdom, knowledge, and understanding from the Holy Spirit, and I am thankful. I can see how my learning grew, my teaching grew, and how my faith grew as a result of this commitment to my faith.

Today, I teach classes for individuals wanting to join the church as adults through RCIA (Rite of Christian Initiation of Adults). The individuals often come with little or no faith background as they are considering joining the Catholic Church. Some are like a blank page with many questions about Catholicism. I often preface their answers to difficult questions by saying, "Here is the crayon version of the answer." The crayon version of an answer is the equivalent of explaining it to them like they are four-year-olds. Start your child's learning at the crayon stage of life, and go back to the crayon stage for yourself if need be. Go to a Catholic bookstore, your priest, or your diocesan office and find the materials that can teach you about the Catholic religion. Not only will you improve your own religion grade, you will receive many fruits for your labor.

---

"When I was a child, I talked like a child, I thought like a child, I reasoned like a child. When I became a man, I put childish ways behind me" (1 Cor. 13:11).

# 23
# The "God Loves Us" Rule

Both my daughters had a pair of Barbie® Princess jeans, and as a mother, I believe there is a time in everyone's life when they should wear Barbie jeans or Winnie the Pooh® jeans (for boys). However, imagine a fifteen-year-old wearing these jeans to high school. It seems silly to suggest this (I hope), but the idea is fashions (along with sizes) change for children as they grow. Furthermore, the meals we prepare for children change as they grow. For example, an eighteen-year-old would probably prefer a McDonald's Big Mac® to a plate of sliced hot dog with ketchup. On the other hand, you would not serve a one-year-old a McDonald's® supersized meal for lunch. St. Paul writes to the people of Corinth, "I fed you milk, not solid food, because you were unable to take it" (1 Cor. 3:2). It only makes sense that as children grow physically, their religious education should grow too. Their spiritual growth will coincide, at a minimum, with their physical and developmental growth.

When children are very young, parents begin teaching about faith through simple stories, like the one about how God made Adam and Eve, or simple songs, such as "Jesus Loves Me." Unfortunately, many do not make it past this beginning stage of faith. It's cute to say simple bedtime prayers with a three-year-old, but not so fun fielding the difficult questions a seventeen-year-old might ask about faith. Parents may feel better equipped to satisfy a three-year-old child's questions about faith with simple answers such as, "Because God loves us."

How and what we teach children about faith needs to be adjusted for—or *grow* with—the child. This sentence seems to state the obvious; however, when teaching about faith, many parents feel unqualified, so they do not teach faith past the elementary level. This is not acceptable. Society would not condone a parent who decided to only teach their child addition and subtraction but not multiplication and division. Society may also tell children mathematics is important because "we use it every day." Catholic parents need to believe the same holds true for faith. We must teach our children past the elementary level, and faith is very important in our daily lives. We use it—or we need it—*every day*.

If you ask a second-grader why we have original sin, you might expect the child to respond, "Because Adam ate the apple." If you ask an eighteen-year-old the same question, you have the right to expect an answer that shows an understanding about Adam's connection to all of humanity, about the free will God gave us, about the impossibility to fully understand and be like God's grace-filled self, and many other answers that show a deeper comprehension and assimilation of the story in life today. Quite simply, as children age, their faith must mature for them to grow as Catholics. Therefore, as the primary teachers of faith to children, parents must also continue to grow in their faith. Growing in faith cannot stop in elementary school, junior high, or high school. It is a lifelong process.

In my classroom, I have a "Because God Loves Us" rule. I was exposed to middle-school students who only had what I called "second-grade answers" to religious questions. They had come to learn that a religion teacher could not say "Because God loves us" was incorrect, and as a result, this became the answer to *each* religion question. Why do we go to confession? Because God loves us. Why do we pray? Because God loves us. Why do we go to Mass? Because God loves us.

If you are promoting growth as a teacher or parent, do not be satisfied with the canned responses and don't always look for just the "right" answers to religion questions. Challenge your children to grow by asking them to go beyond the canned response. For example, follow up a "God loves us" response with "How does that show God's love?" If they can't go deeper than the canned response, find an answer yourself and then model it to them. Whether you start your learning with a children's Bible or an adult version, learn to answer faith questions beyond the canned responses so that you can promote good faith discussion and spiritual growth.

Working past the canned responses takes practice. When my children came home from school and I asked, "What did you do at school today?" they tried to give me the canned response, "Nothin'." Perhaps you have had this interaction a time or two.

When I receive this response from my children, I go into a pretend tirade about how terrible their school is that sounds something like this: "Well, I better call your school, because I am paying them to teach you something every day. I can't believe you spent eight hours at that place and they couldn't teach you one thing. I better let your principal know what is going on in your classroom."

As a result of my reaction, my children quickly learned that I was committed to their education and I was very interested in what they were learning. Also, as a result, we have had many great conversations about what was going on at school because I did not let them get away with the canned response.

When my children said they did nothing in school, it usually meant they were not really interested in a conversation about it. Similarly, when students give me a "God loves us" response, it may mean they aren't interested in a conversation about faith or they don't know how to have a conversation about it. A pretend tirade that can be used to encourage discussion might sound like this: "Oh my, God gave us this Bible that tells us of so many ways He loves us, and we can't even recall one! We better start reading this book until we can find some answers about how much God loves us. Let's get our Bibles out and start reading right now. I don't want to disappoint God." At this point, you must commit to start reading or be prepared to be amazed by what your child might share. Either way, you will be sharing faith and you both will grow in the process.

If I ask my students about the school dress code or homework, they can express their feelings in many different ways; however, when I ask about their feelings on a scripture passage, they seem a bit uncomfortable and much less vocal. Scripture is not the usual topic of their adolescent conversations. When I began teaching seventh-graders how to reflect on scripture, their responses often started very canned and shallow. So, I started with some guidelines you can use in getting past such responses with your children.

Practice sitting in uncomfortable silence. This was a hard thing for me to learn how to do, but it has provided me with incredible comments from children who just needed time to process things since they are inexperienced at it.

Give instructions that there are no wrong answers to how scripture makes you feel or what it means to you in a particular moment. We train children to always look for the one right answer in school when we give them tests, but how scripture works within us cannot be packaged into neat little multiple-choice questions. There is no wrong response when children are asked to tell what word or phrase from the scripture stands out to them. There are only opportunities to grow from a question like this.

Give children answers, ask them to choose, and have them tell why they chose the answer they chose. For example, I might ask each student to hold up their fingers to represent their answer to the question. "On a scale of one to five, how much do you agree with what is being said?" I have asked students if Jesus was more like a small creek, some whitewater rapids, or an ocean. Once they commit, I ask them to explain. You can't answer, "Because God loves me" to these questions.

Ask the question, "What did you not understand about this scripture passage?" or "What do you agree/disagree with in this passage?" You could ask, "Why do you think it should be okay to only confess our sins directly to God and not to a priest?" Again, there is no wrong answer, and such questions are very nonthreatening to children. It actually makes them feel their opinion counts, and if you ever ask them about the dress code or homework policy, they clearly demonstrate how much they want their opinion heard.

Ask open-ended questions about faith, such as, "What would you have done if you were Peter and the people were attacking you for knowing Jesus?" or "Why do you think we shouldn't have to go to Mass on Sundays?" Meanwhile, let them know in advance that the answer, "Because God loves us" is not enough. When you can have a real discussion about faith, scripture, or religion that goes beyond, "God loves us," you start the conversation and you both learn.

I should conclude by saying that technically, "God loves us" *is* the answer to every religion question. However, if this is the only answer (and especially if it is simply a canned response) a Catholic child can provide, it sets the stage for the Catholic child to become ... well ... *taller*.

# 24
# Carrots or Potato Chips?

Just as children's appetites grow with their physical bodies, so too must their hunger and appetite for faith. This hunger will come from what you feed them.

Left to their own devices, many two-year-olds (and perhaps eighteen-year-olds) would have a bag of potato chips, a soda, and a chocolate bar for lunch. Generally, parents would not encourage this type of lunch. It is one of the "mean" jobs we get to have as parents: making children eat healthy food. Parents do this out of love, so children will grow to be strong and healthy and develop good eating habits. Also out of love, parents should monitor what is being "fed" to their children spiritually. This, too, will help them to grow to be strong, healthy, and happy.

Often, we hear parents tell children, "You must eat to grow, and if you eat healthy food, you will grow to be big and strong." The same applies to spiritual growth: it must be fed, and it must be served healthy ingredients. More important, if you are not the one feeding them spiritually, you should be very concerned about who is.

I have taught junior high and high school Catholic students who have told me they were "fed" the line, "You do not have to receive the sacrament of reconciliation," and "Jesus really isn't present in Communion." They have been asked, "Are you saved?" and been frightened because their Protestant friends tell them they must be saved to get to Heaven. Consider the disheartening but very honest words spoken by Dr. Scott Hahn on his video, *Scott Hahn's Conversion Story*.[4] Mr. Hahn is a former Protestant minister who later converted to Catholicism and was once a self-proclaimed "anti-Catholic."

> [My four years of college] I devoted myself to reaching unchurched kids who didn't know about Christ. And I confess that this category included Catholic kids in the high school where I worked, because I looked at these poor benighted souls as people who didn't really know Jesus Christ. And I discovered after several Bible studies that not only did these kids not know Jesus Christ, but practically every Catholic high school kid I met didn't even know what the Catholic Church taught. And if one or two of them knew what the Church taught, they didn't know why. They didn't have any reasons to back up their beliefs as Catholics. So, getting them to see from the Bible the Gospel as I understood it from Martin Luther—from an anti-Catholic perspective—was like picking off ducks in a barrel. They weren't ready; they were unequipped. They were defenseless. I don't know exactly what has happened in the last 15–20–25 years, but I look back on those kids and wonder if they weren't guinea pigs in some sort of catechetical experiment that people thought we could bypass instructing them in the doctrines they need to believe and the reasons for those doctrines. But here they were, and I saw many of them leave the Church.

Dr. Hahn's experience was my own experience, and research provides further support. The NFCYM data reported only 34 percent of Catholic youth and their families talk about God, the scriptures, prayer, or other religious or spiritual things together *once a week or more*, and 19 percent responded that they "never" discuss these topics. Just as Dr. Hahn discovered in his college days, a majority of Catholic parents today are leaving the "feeding" of their children's spiritual hunger to others.

The good news from the NFCYM data is that teens are "hungry" because 74 percent reported to be somewhat or very interested in learning more about their religion. This may come as a surprise to many Catholic parents today because spiritual hunger is not seen on the surface. Physical hunger—say that of a starving child in Africa—is very

---

4   St. Joseph Communications, West Covina, CA, 1996.

evident; spiritual hunger is not. How parents nourish this hunger for spirituality is equally as important as the food they feed their children. Therefore, if you want to grow Catholic children, you must feed them Catholic tradition and scripture.

This doesn't mean you can't discuss other faiths and religions, but it does mean you need to be there to help them explore. My son grew tremendously in his faith when his non-Catholic friends challenged his faith and we searched for answers together. Any study of faith will undoubtedly lead to spiritual growth. It is what led to the conversion of Dr. Scott Hahn. His book, *Rome Sweet Home,* is the perfect example of how study brings people to the truth. It is also a book I strongly recommend. Study is what turned me from a nonpracticing Catholic to a relentless Catholic mother. In summary, the only way to be sure of what your children are being fed spiritually is to be the one to feed it to them. Otherwise, don't be surprised if they abandon their faith as Dr. Hahn describes.

You feed your children spiritually by having the religious conversations with them as discussed in the last chapter. Simply put:

- Make time each day to talk about faith with your children.
- Study and learn about faith with your children.
- Constantly model the faith to your children.
- Pray *for* and *with* your children.

If you need to feed your own spirituality:

- Make time each day to read scripture or other religious books and discuss your readings with others of faith.
- Study and learn from your diocese, church, priest, religious, or church employees and volunteers.
- Surround yourself with people who model the faith.
- Pray for knowledge and spiritual growth.

---

"I am the bread of life … This is the bread that comes down from out of heaven, so that one may eat of it and not die. I am the living bread that came down out of heaven; if anyone eats of this bread, he will live forever" (John 6:48–51).

# 25
# I'm Not Qualified

Martin Pable, in an article, "Why Don't Catholics Share Their Faith,"[5] identifies three reasons for the reluctance to share faith: 1) Catholics have heard stories of immigrant parents who were discriminated against for being Catholic, 2) Catholics have come to accept the American value of pluralism—"live and let live," and 3) what I believe to be the most important reason, "many contemporary Catholics have grown up without clear knowledge of their beliefs and what underlies them so they feel inadequate to explain or defend them if challenged." Mr. Pable goes on to say, "Add to this the fallout from the sexual abuse scandals including the loss of credibility of Church authorities and you have a multitude of reasons why Catholics find it daunting to share their faith in public ways, and anyway isn't one's religion a private matter?"

Just as Jesus called the first disciples to follow him (Matt. 4:19), so are parents called to be disciples. Through the baptismal promises you made at your child's baptism, you made the commitment before your Catholic community and God to do exactly that. Sharing with your children gives you experience and practice so you may share with others as we are all called to do. Jesus says in Mark 16:15, "Go into all the world and preach the Gospel to all creation." What makes you think He was not speaking to you? Or what makes you think you are exempt from this call from Jesus? In this passage, He is speaking to all of us, even those of us living over two thousand years after His death.

---

5  *America* (Volume 193, No. 7, New York: America Press, Inc., 2005).

How awesome is it we share in the same ministry as those first called by Jesus? I am thankful those first disciples did not keep it private, and now I must do the same.

As I mentioned, my family was very private about our faith. We were very good at being Catholic in private but were afraid to share. It wasn't until about ten years ago that I fully understood my need to share. I was preparing to give a talk about the layperson in the church. In meditating and researching my theme, I realized two things. First, I learned that I am not doing enough by just bringing faith to my own children. We all belong to God's family and are children of God; therefore, all people are the children I must bring faith to. There were times when I thought writing this book would be arrogant or about building up my own ego. Now I realize it is about following God's command to preach to all for His glory.

The second thing I learned in preparing my presentation was that I actually do bring faith to others in the little things I do. Each time I listen to someone who is struggling, I am being a qualified witness and sharing faith. I learned I was qualified by my desire to show Christ's love to others, and I began to share more. It was not easy, and I still slip up from time to time. When I am successful as a witness, it is because I am open to the graces God has for me. I stop and offer thanks to him. When I stumble, God's grace is still there; I am just not open to seeing it.

For example, when a store clerk forgot to charge me for some items and I went back to pay the difference, I was a qualified witness. When I overheard someone gossiping about a mutual acquaintance and said nothing to prevent it, I was not acting as a qualified witness. In both examples, I was a witness by my actions. I was well qualified to do the right thing in both instances because I had read about how to treat my neighbor in the Bible.

I had my children baptized because I wanted them to share in the joy that comes from a life of faith and a relationship with Christ. I also want them to experience the joy of everlasting life in heaven. I understand my responsibility with my own children, but God said my responsibility does not stop there. I need to desire that joy for *all* the people of God, and I need to know that *I* play a role in getting them there, but I started with my own family and challenge you to start with yours.

Feeling unqualified, however, is not something saved exclusively for parents. Know you are not alone in your uncertainty. Take two examples of Old Testament figures who felt unsure of their ability to spread the Word of God. We only know of them as very qualified prophets, but they did not always feel that way.

For example, take the response of the prophet Jeremiah when he was called by the Lord at the age of thirteen. "'Ah, Lord God!' I said, 'I know not how to speak; I am too young'" (Jer. 1:4). When the Lord called Moses to go to Pharaoh to lead the Israelites out of Egypt, Moses replied, "Who am I that I should go …?" (Exod. 3:11). What these great prophets failed to realize at the moment of their calling was that God was going to give them the words to speak. In fact, God answered Moses, "I will be with you …" (Exod. 3:12). The same holds true for you as a parent, but like Jeremiah and Moses, you must first have an open and willing heart. Moses and Jeremiah showed us that being an expert, or being qualified, is not a requirement to share God's Word. Having a desire to do God's will is required. Jesus even uses a lowly, adulterous Samaritan woman to catechize the town of Samaria. What she had, and what parents must have, is a passion for sharing the faith.

These three examples teach us the important lesson that God does not just call the qualified; he qualifies the called. There is a difference. Many Catholic parents are guilty of feeling inadequate about sharing faith or feeling ill-prepared to preach the Gospel. Truthfully, all humans are unqualified to *fully* reveal the kingdom of heaven or the love of God the Father. Even Jesus could not always get the message through to his followers. In the Gospel of John, Jesus tells His followers, "'Amen, amen, I say to you, unless you eat the flesh of the Son of Man and drink his blood, you do not have life within you.' … many of his disciples returned to their former way of life and no longer accompanied him" (John 6:53, 66). Even though Jesus lost followers on this day, His example to us was to keep preaching.

Catholics can no longer be shy about sharing faith. For the future of the Catholic faith and the happiness of our children, we cannot afford to be. Catholics must share faith with the whole world by telling the stories and passing on Catholic tradition as Jesus asked us to do. This important mission belongs to us all. Perhaps those first apostles were thinking as I do from time to time, "It is a very scary world out there." As laypersons in the church, we represent the largest percent of the people of God. We cannot merely rely on priests and the religious to spread the Good News. Eventually, we must go beyond our families, but for now, who better to start sharing with than your own children? They are a very nonthreatening audience for practicing your evangelization skills. In your car, on your trip to and from church, they are also a captive audience. Use these minutes to share faith. On the drive to church, talk about the readings that will be read during the Liturgy of the Word, discuss the feast day, or simply ask questions such as, "Where did you see Christ this week?" On the drive home, talk about the homily or the readings. Talk to them about how you have seen God or how your faith has helped you. If this is hard to do, start by opening your own heart like Jeremiah and Moses. If you allow God to use you as His instrument, you will be more than qualified to do His work. Being honest is another key to successful conversation. If you had a difficult time finding God this week, let them know that. This still offers an opportunity for conversation and growth.

The following text provides a good reminder for all parents:

### *Something to Remember*

The next time you feel like God can't or wouldn't want to use you, just remember:

> "Noah was a drunk, Abraham was very old, Isaac was a daydreamer, Jacob was a liar, Joseph was abused, Moses had a stuttering problem, Samson had long hair and was a womanizer, Rahab was a prostitute, Jeremiah and Timothy were very young, David had an affair and was a murderer, Elijah was suicidal, Isaiah preached naked, Jonah ran from God, Naomi was a widow, Job went bankrupt, John the Baptist ate bugs, Peter denied Christ (three times), the disciples fell asleep while praying, Martha was a worry wart, the Samaritan woman was divorced (more than once), Zaccheus was very small, and Lazarus was DEAD. Now what makes you think God can't or wouldn't use you?"

Author Unknown

---

"I can do all things through Him who strengthens me" (Phil. 4:13).

# 26
# Why Do Catholics Do That?

A big part of feeling qualified to share faith is to know some answers to the question presented in this title. Catholics are infamous for their inability to share their faith publicly. When a Protestant starts spouting Bible versus at us, we start squirming in our seats. Someone asks a Catholic to look something up in the Bible, and they start flipping through pages randomly, asking, "Is that book in the front or the back of the Bible?"

If you really want to confound a Catholic, merely ask, "Why do Catholics do that?"

Typically, they will answer, "That's just the way we do it," or "I don't know. That's what my mom taught me to do."

Unfortunately, these answers are clearly not enough for today's children.

As we saw from Scott Hahn's experience and my own, if children can't defend their faith, they are too easily swayed away from it. Unlike saying, "Because God loves us," which is a true statement, it is not true to say, "That is just the way we do it" when asked why. It is also not enough to respond this way because there is meaning behind why Catholics do what they do. Understand the meaning behind why Catholics do what they do and receive the joy that comes from knowing. Then go share that joy.

If I were to ask, "Why does Chicago Cubs right fielder and slugger Sammy Sosa pound his chest twice, kiss his first two fingers, and point to the sky after hitting a home run?" I believe many Catholics could give an answer to this question. And believe it or not, the answer to this question is the same as the answer to the question, "Why do Catholics do that?" The answer is because it has meaning. Once you learn Sammy makes this gesture to acknowledge his mother in Heaven, it gives those seemingly random motions importance. The ritual becomes meaningful, and now, with understanding, we can support him doing this and perhaps even get joy upon seeing it.

One of your roles as a parent and as a disciple of Christ is to know the answers to the question, "Why do Catholics do that?" The answers are found in many places and through many people. Do the research; ask the questions. If someone, especially your child, asks you, "Why do Catholics do that?" and the only immediate answer you have is something like, "That's just the way we do it," then know you are not fulfilling your baptismal promises. None of us has all the answers, but we all have the ability to find them. Make the commitment to find the answers.

Today, I have absolute confidence in saying two things: 1) I do not fully understand everything I need to now about faith, the stories in the Bible, or God's grace, and 2) I must continually challenge myself to better understand my faith. This is the example we must give children. We cannot rest on our laurels and only teach them, "Jesus loves the little children" or "God loves us." Instead, we need to say, "I'm not sure, but let's find out the answer to that question," and then do it. Ask a priest or a religious. Consult books you can understand. Do this research *with them*. It is not enough to say, "Go ask your teacher," and send them off alone. By answering the question, "Why do Catholics do that?" *together*, you *both* grow.

# Part VI
# Surround and Share

*"Just so, your light must shine before others, that they may see your good deeds and glorify your heavenly Father"* (Matt. 5:16).

☙

# 27
# How to Sell Your Home to a Catholic in Ninety Days

A few years ago, my husband and I had a difficult time selling our home. We consulted realtors and got a lot of advice. We removed clutter to make the house seem more open and clean. We had several prospective buyers walk through our home but had no offers. Then, one day, my husband stood in our front room and said, "Well, the realtors are probably bringing prospective buyers who are not Catholic to our home, and we could never sell this home to anyone who isn't Catholic." This seems like an odd statement, but upon glancing around our home from this vantage point, my husband observed a holy water font in the foyer, pictures of the Pope and Last Supper on the wall, a scapular and palms tucked away behind crucifixes on the wall, my collection of saint figurines in the dining room hutch, a Bible and other religious books on the coffee table, and a few other items, but I don't think I need to continue for you to get the point.

Look around your home. What does your decor say about your family? Do you have religious items on display? Does your family own a Bible or a Rosary? If so, are they readily available to be used, or are they stuffed in a drawer or a closet somewhere in your home? Does your Catholic home display a picture of the Last Supper? Do you put out a nativity scene during the Christmas season, or do you fill your home with only Santa Claus images?

My youngest daughter was learning about the Rosary in school.

She came home and told me, "I told my teacher our family is very holy because we have fourteen Rosaries." I explained to her that having religious items in your home does not make you a holy person. It is your words and deeds that make you holy. Nor do you have to have these items on display to be a holy person. Holiness existed long before fancy pictures of the Last Supper. The idea is to make religion part of your environment so it can become part of your life.

As a marketing major in college, I was taught about a concept called *top-of-mind awareness*. The idea is to promote something often enough it becomes the first thing to come to a buyer's mind when he or she is making a purchase. Obtaining top-of-mind awareness requires having your product or service in the sight of the consumer a particular number of times. All anyone has to do to believe this concept is watch an hour of television and see how many times a commercial is shown.

Having religious articles in my home accomplishes two things. One, they serve as little and needed reminders for my family to make faith a part of our day (top-of-mind-awareness). I make a point to look at something every day to remind me to put the love of Christ in my heart that day. For a while, it was a picture of Jesus made up of several images of other people's faces that motivated me. It reminded me all people have Christ in them and should be treated accordingly. It could be a prayer, a favorite Bible verse on your bathroom mirror, or a picture of the Last Supper. The second thing religious articles in your home can do is evangelize to others. Those entering our home know something about how important our faith is, and many religious conversations I never would have expected to have with strangers have taken place in my home as a result of a religious item. Who knows? A conversation could have taken place in my absence between a realtor and a prospective buyer. Now that's evangelization!

As humans, we often need to see and touch things before they seem real. Our liturgy and our churches are full of symbols and rituals to help us remember, appreciate, and evangelize our faith. Perhaps Jesus, who gave us the Mass, knew about top-of-the-mind awareness. Religious articles in my home have made a difference in my life. I challenge you to try one on for size.

---

"As for me and my household, we will serve the Lord" (Josh. 24:15).

# 28
# Sticks and Stones May Break My Bones

Perhaps you have heard this familiar adage, the conclusion of which is, "but names will never hurt me." This is a great tool for dealing with name-calling, but it does not adequately address the name-caller. When I was in high school, I took a job working at a fast-food restaurant. The manager and several employees were accustomed to using profanity on a regular basis. At work, I was constantly surrounded by this language until it became so commonplace I hardly noticed it. One day, I noticed myself using one of the cuss words often said by other employees and wondered how many times I had said this particular word without even noticing. This gave me (and my mother who had overheard me using the word) a time for pause. In that moment, I realized that although I hadn't gone out of my way to include cuss words in my conversations, they had just become part of my vocabulary through my exposure to such language and by my being in an environment that accepted and tolerated it.

There are plenty of movies, Web sites, and music and television programs that do not include God's Word or message. As a parent, you have an obligation to know what messages your children are listening to or watching each day and hold them accountable for it. It seems impossible to shelter our children from all non-Christian messages, but you must not promote such messages by letting them convince you,

"It is only a TV show," or "Everybody else watches it or listens to it." Each year, I ask my students to print the lyrics for one of their favorite songs and write about them, and each year, students are surprised at the messages they find in the lyrics they are listening to. The United States Council of Catholic Bishops provides a Web site, www.usccb.org, which gives the moral rating of movies the secular world says are acceptable for children. Become familiar with this resource for movie information, daily scripture readings, and much more helpful information. This is one way to find Christ's message from the Internet.

In an attempt to justify the movies they watch or the music they listen to, my children and students have tried to convince me cuss words are just words. They protest, "Words don't mean anything."

From my experience, however, the reality is words say something about the person speaking them. For example, my grandmother used to always say, "God love her," all the time. When we did something sweet, she'd say, "God love her." When we got in trouble, she'd say, "God love her," to our mother to summon sympathy. When we were sad or crying, she'd say, "God love her," and offer a hug. I believe if this was all I told you about my grandmother, you would be able to make an impression of the type of person she was. It certainly makes sense to conclude I grew to know more about God by being with my grandmother than I ever will learn from listening to a rap song, watching a movie, or being around an employer with profane language.

Other than religious articles, there are many other things to surround yourself with to help you grow in faith. I believe the most important thing is God's Word. We are surrounded by God's words at Mass, and we can submerse ourselves in the Bible through daily readings. I began attending more than the Sunday Eucharist. I started reading the Bible daily. Sometimes I read from a children's Bible or a youth Bible, and sometimes I read from a good adult Bible with many references and footnotes. I started with the children's books of popular Bible stories. In my adult Bible, I began with the four Gospels. I did not start by reading from page one of Genesis through to the last page of Revelation, and I did not attempt to tackle too much in a day. I found a book with daily Catholic devotions at www.livingfaith.com and a liturgical desk calendar from I. Donnelly Company, Inc., published by Franklin X. McCormick, Inc., with the daily scripture readings. By surrounding myself with God's Word, I became a better teacher of the faith for my children; I became more qualified to witness. By sharing God's Word with others in religious conversations, I became a growing Catholic. If you are intimidated by the Bible, just begin with these five steps:

1) Pray to the Holy Spirit to help you hear God's Word prior to reading.
2) Read a Bible passage.
3) Read any footnotes or look up any cross-references.
4) Reread the passage.
5) Meditate on what you just read, asking questions, such as "What word or phrase stuck out to me? What message is God trying to send me? Where do I see myself in this passage? What is this passage calling me to do *today* in my life?" You will discover the words in the Bible are words that *do* mean something. And yes, they certainly can be hard to hear when God is telling us we need to change.

Outside God's written words in the Bible, I surround myself with his words by frequently listening to a Christian radio station that proclaims scripture and plays music that speaks of Christ's love. There are times when the messages from this radio station have changed my mood for the day. If I start my day with a hectic morning, this radio station can relax me on my morning drive to work and leave me feeling hopeful and uplifted by the time I start my work day.

The other radio station I often listen to is a talk radio station that offers the news, information, and weather. Although I enjoy this station, it is often hard to be uplifted by the sometimes depressing news stories or weather reports. The words of the Bible, however, never fail to inspire. Find a Christian radio station for your drive time and preset the station. If you find yourself in a situation where you need to be encouraged, take it for a test drive. You will not be disappointed.

I encourage you to evaluate the messages with which you surround yourself and your children. If you are tempted to argue that words don't mean anything, then try exposing yourself to the words found in your Bible. Read a passage from the Bible each day. Find a Christian radio station or television program to listen to, or simply listen to these words at church. I know surrounding yourself with the right words will give meaning to your life.

---

"Amen, amen, I say to you, whoever hears my word and believes in the one who sent me has eternal life and will not come to condemnation …" (John 5:24).

# 29
# Frank or Frances?

In addition to surrounding yourself with God's Word, spend time with religious and prayerful people. I did not say perfect people or living saints, but simply people who believe in Christ and are not afraid to share. There are religious and prayerful people alive and dead (the saints); they are encountered face-to-face, on television, and in the movies. If you do not know religious or prayerful people, volunteer at your church or attend a retreat. I will give you a 100 percent guarantee that you will find some at these two places. I have encouraged my children and husband to attend Catholic retreats because I knew it would give them the opportunity to be surrounded by religious people. Never once did any of them come back saying they hated the experience or the people. Rather, what resulted was tremendous growth in their faith. My husband also says that assisting me with CCD classes was a time of growth for him too. It has done tremendous things for our relationship as well. He is my perfect reminder that you can't outgive God.

There is a beautiful memoir written by Frank McCourt titled, *Angela's Ashes*. It is a sad story of an Irish family living during the Great Depression and struggling with disease, poverty, hunger, death, and alcoholism. Mr. McCourt himself says, "My brother and I wonder how we survived." However, as I read this book, I couldn't help but find myself somewhat jealous of the fact that Mr. McCourt lived in a place and time where his religion and Catholic identity were woven into the fabric of his daily living through the people around him. Mr. McCourt describes in his book how the children knew it was time to come in from playing when they heard the church Angelus bells ring. He recounts how neighbors and store owners contributed food to his family because they understood Catholic social justice that says we must feed the hungry and respect the dignity of all life. In another example, a shopkeeper asks a young Mr. McCourt his name, and he responds, "Frank." The shopkeeper goes on to explain that his name can't be Frank because there is no Saint Frank. Further he states that the young boy's name must be Frances, for Saint Frances. In my opinion, through the sharing of their Catholic identity, these people are part of the answer to Mr. McCourt's question of how he survived.

Unfortunately, in our world today, our children face many challenges finding Catholic role models. This is why it is especially important that you are one. As parents, teachers of faith, and Christians, you must promote the existence of faith at all opportunities. For example, when my students ask me, "What do I get for helping pass out papers?"

I simply quote the Bible and say, "Your reward will be great in heaven" (Matt. 5:12). On another occasion, I might say, "You will receive the joy of knowing you just made God smile today."

As disappointed as they seem at the time, they *never* argue the point further. Like the shopkeeper in Frank McCourt's life, my comments provide a small reminder of their Catholic identity. In a previous chapter, I mentioned my home has reminders of my Catholic identity, but I also bring that identity to the people I run into at the supermarket by being kind. I bring it to my family when I send a prayer card tucked inside a religious-themed Christmas card or when I tell someone I will pray for them.

I have met with converted prisoners who say when they leave prison, they are unable to return to the people who were a part of the life that led them to prison. Sadly, this sometimes means giving up contact with family and friends who tempt them with drugs, profanity, and crime. These prisoners have clearly learned the value of surrounding themselves with prayerful people and God's Word during their conversions. They have seen the pain that comes from their previous life and the joy that comes from their conversion. Much like these prisoners, we must all look at the people we surround ourselves with and determine if they are helping us grow in faith or keeping us from it. For those who are not helping *you* to grow, perhaps you can help them to grow by bringing your Catholic identity to them. If you work in a place that allows it, a religious picture or figurine can help you surround yourself with your faith.

I have a prayer group that meets weekly to discuss God's work in our lives. We pray together, encourage one another, challenge one another, inspire one another, comfort one another, and sometimes just listen to one another. We enjoy laughter and sharing in a Christian setting. The more I am around this group and others like them, the more faithful and joyful a Christian I become. I study the lives of the saints, receive inspiration from their stories, and find comfort when I call on their intercession. I watch movies about holy people and some with religious themes. I feel truly blessed for all the holy people in my life, including the communion of saints, living and dead.

When I say I am surrounded by the communion of saints, I am including my collection of saint figurines. I began collecting saints about five years ago because I wanted to know more about them and my husband informed me I needed to start collecting something so he would have a standard gift to buy for me on birthdays and other occasions. As my collection grew, something amazing happened. I began to come to know their stories by the information and prayer card packaged with each saint. Then, not surprisingly, I made my husband purchase the book, *Butler's Lives of the Saints* for me one Christmas so I could learn even more.

I discovered by surrounding myself with these saints and their stories that it was possible for me to be a saint by how I live my life. Even with all the mistakes of my past, there was hope for me still. I also learned that we are all called to be saints, and the more I learned about their lives, the more I wanted to be like them. By surrounding myself with these holy people, I have become a better Catholic. This is the purpose of the saints in the Catholic Church. We do not worship them as some may believe, but we use their lives as examples of how to love God and live holy lives.

Chances are you have holy people in your life. Surround yourself with their example. Just like the saints our Church has canonized over the years, the holy people in your life will not be perfect, but use these canonized and non-canonized saints to teach you how to be a holy person.

Of course, I do find myself in the company of non-religious people. Catholics need to meet those in the secular world who believe contrary to our faith in order to share our faith with them, but having an "army" of religious and prayerful people behind us helps guarantee our success in growing as Catholics and helping others grow.

# 30
# American Idol

Children are taught early on to share their toys, but not everyone is taught to share his or her gifts from God. God is the creator of all life, and every gift we have comes from Him. Not sharing your gifts with those around you is like asking for a refund from God. A father might feel the need to return an ugly tie he received for Father's Day, but the gifts bestowed upon us by God are perfect. God is the perfect gift giver, no refunds necessary. Learn to accept the gifts God has given you, and share them with those around you.

Each gift He has given you is to be used to glorify Him. As St. Paul writes in Romans 12:6:

> Since we have gifts that differ according to the grace given to us, let us exercise them: if prophecy, in proportion to the faith; if ministry, in ministering; if one is a teacher, in teaching; if one exhorts, in exhortation; if one contributes, in generosity; if one is over other, with diligence; if one does acts of mercy, with cheerfulness.

When we share God's gifts, we bring joy to those with whom we share. We also bring joy to ourselves.

For example, when I watch the television program, *American Idol*, I get great joy listening to the talented singers and musicians as they share their gifts, and it is obvious the contestants on this program also receive much joy in sharing these gifts. They speak about it in interviews. This mutual joy in the sharing of these gifts is how we know these gifts are from God. The contestants may never fully know the joy they give me or others through their singing, but they do know their calling. That is what is important.

Know that everyone has a gift to offer. To deny you have any gifts is to say our creator made a mistake. If you are having trouble finding your gift, just listen to those around you. People are happy to identify your gifts for you. I constantly nag my oldest daughter to share her gift of singing because she has this gift from God. (She absolutely did not inherit this from her parents.) My nagging is a case of me identifying her gift for her.

Prior to my serious consideration of publishing my writing, I prayed for God to speak to me about my calling for the gifts he has given me. Within two days, I had about four people tell me I should write. One even told me I need to publish my poems. These were all rather random comments, and they were not the usual comments made by my husband who is constantly telling me His gift on earth is to encourage me to write and bring this book to fruition! So when I say to listen to others, you don't even necessarily have to ask about your gifts, just be prepared to listen and hear what they identify for you. Then go share that gift; it is part of God's plan.

Another way to identify your gifts is to think of the things that bring joy into your life. Chances are if you receive joy in sharing it, it is God's gift for you. Each time I share my spiritual gifts with others, I receive blessings in return. What other gift giver can truly give you a gift that keeps on giving?

The following are some examples of gifts you can share besides your toys:

- Share your God-given talents with the church (music, speaking, writing, teaching, organizing, leading, budgeting, hospitality, artistry, etc.).
- Share the peace and joy Christ has given you with others by being a peaceful and joyful person.
- Share your treasure by giving back to God a portion of what He has blessed you with financially.
- Share your knowledge and love of faith with all people.
- Share your kindness with a lonely person.

- Share your love with all.
- Share your patience with a small child or an elderly or handicapped person.
- Share your forgiveness with a hurtful person.
- Share your understanding with a difficult person.
- Share your time with someone who needs to see Christ in his or her world today.
- Share your smile with all you meet today.

This should get you started. Now go share!

---

"He sat down opposite the treasury and observed how the crowd put money into the treasury. Many rich people put in large sums. A poor widow also came and put in two small coins worth a few cents. Calling his disciples to himself, he said to them, 'Amen, I say to you, this poor widow put in more than all the other contributors to the treasury. For they have all contributed from their surplus wealth, but she, from her poverty, has contributed all she had, her whole livelihood'" (Mark 12:41–44).

# 31
## The Little Red Hen

The old children's story "The Little Red Hen" reminds me of our responsibility to go on our faith journey and serve. It started as a story I would retell to my children many times because it had a good message. Eventually, we all had the story memorized, and I would merely have to say, "Have I told you the story of 'The Little Red Hen'?" for them to get the message (and throw a couple groans my way). It was especially useful in getting my children to share in a household chore like getting supper ready. Then one day, it became the perfect parable for everlasting life.

If you are not familiar with the story, allow me to summarize. In the story, the hen finds some grains of wheat. She asks for help from all the farm animals to plant the wheat, cut the wheat, take the wheat to the miller to be ground into flour, make dough from the flour, and bake the bread. At every step in this process, the hen asks, "Who will help me?"

Each time, all the farm animals say, "Not I."

At the very end of the story, when the hen asks, "Who will help me eat this bread?"

All the animals reply, "I will." The story ends with the hen eating all the bread alone with her baby chicks.

There is more to learn from this story than to be helpful to others. Just like the little red hen, Christ led by example. He planted the seeds and labored for the harvest. The little red hen sacrificed much time and energy in order to enjoy bread. She invited the other farm animals to share in her labor. Christ made sacrifices in order for us to share in the Kingdom of God. Today, He invites us to do the same when he tells us, "No one comes to the Father except through me" (John 14:6). He is asking us to follow his example. Many Catholics are willing to have faith in Christ, but they are like the farm animals in the story. They want the reward of the bread without sharing in the labor. They are unwilling to work for their reward. As Catholics, we must be willing to enter fully into the sacrifices of Christ with Him.

A priest once expressed this message in a homily by telling the parable of a tightrope walker who was preparing to walk across Niagara Falls without a net. Spectators watched and cheered, "We have faith you can do it!"

After he successfully crossed the falls, he asked, "Do you believe I can do it blindfolded?"

They all cheered him on again, saying, "Yes, we have faith in you!"

The man completed this task successfully. The crowd cheered. Then, the man asked, "Do you believe I can do it while carrying a man on my shoulders?"

The crowd roared again, "Yes, we have faith in you!"

So, the tightrope walker asked, "Do I have any volunteers?"

The crowd fell silent. Many were willing to have faith but not willing to sacrifice. Think about where you stand on your willingness to *work* for Christ. The Bible says, "What good is it, my brothers, if someone says he has faith but does not have works? … For just as a body without a spirit is dead, so also faith without works is dead" (James 2:14, 26).

Sharing in Christ's work means serving others. Christ washed the feet of the disciples. Though we call him "Master," he had no servants. Quite simply, He came to earth to serve. Never have I been in service for the Lord and not received a greater gift than the gift of service I provided, especially in my service to the church. For example, I have grown more in faith by serving others as a teacher, and I have learned so much about sacred scripture by serving as a lector in my church. I encourage you to serve others and your church, and be prepared to grow.

My children have heard me say, "Look backward," many times in their lives. I use it to help them understand their obligation to give and to serve. When they complain about needing material things "because everyone else has one," I ask them to think about the people who have less than they do. Often, they have "looked forward" at others who have more than they do. When this happens, I challenge them to look behind them and see those who have less than they do. There is *always* someone who has less.

I cried when my oldest daughter and I purchased Easter basket goodies at a local dollar store for the poor in our community. I was moved when she and I made a warm breakfast of eggs and pancakes for the homeless at Thanksgiving, and we both learned an important lesson on acceptance by volunteering for the Special Olympics. In all these instances, it was very easy for us to look backward at those less fortunate and appreciate what we truly have. Serving others provides you with opportunities to humbly appreciate all the blessings God has bestowed on you. When we become counters of blessings, we grow in faith. Your reward for service, though not material, will be priceless.

I challenge you to go out and serve and take your children with you. Don't simply take up a monetary collection. Go see the faces of the poor and visit the sick. A canned food drive for the poor is great, but each time I introduce my children or my students to the recipients of the food drive, the benefits to their spiritual growth are exponential.

The idea of putting a face on those you serve reminds me of a line from the movie *Good Will Hunting* that makes the message even clearer. Actor Robin Williams plays a psychological counselor working with a brilliant book scholar who is struggling with real life. He confronts him with the following words, "So if I asked you about art, you'd probably give me the skinny on every art book ever written. Michelangelo, you know a lot about him. Life's work, political aspirations, him and the Pope, sexual orientations, the whole works, right? But I'll bet you can't tell me what it smells like in the Sistine Chapel. You've never actually stood there and looked up at that beautiful ceiling."

In our world today, Christ is in need of those willing to share in His work. In the words of St. Teresa of Avilla, "Christ has no body now, but ours. No hands, no feet on earth, but ours. Ours are the eyes through which He looks with compassion on this world. Ours are the feet with which He walks to do good. Ours are the hands with which He blesses all the world. Ours are the hands, ours are the feet, ours are the eyes, we are His body." St. Paul says the baptized have "clothed yourselves with Christ" (Gal. 3:27). You may be the only Christ some people see in their lives. Don't miss the opportunity to discover the joy that comes from sharing in His work.

Christ is the living bread of eternal life. He offers his bread freely to each of us through His sacrifice on the cross *and* asks us to follow Him. To follow Him means we should simply ask the question, "What would Jesus do?" and then go do it. In short, are you willing to serve?

---

"The harvest is abundant but the laborers are few" (Luke 10:2).

# Part VII
# Grow

*Prepare to Be Changed*

☙

# 32
# Raising the Bar

When imagining the raising of an object, most imagine an object being moved to a higher plane. Even metaphorically, the term "raising the bar" means setting something higher—higher goals, higher expectations, etc. So when I think of Catholic parents *raising* their children, I wonder, "Is the outcome to be a generation of Catholics who are simply taller, or should we hope to create a generation of Catholics who are continually *growing* in their faith?" Having been *raised* Catholic, I would argue the outcome should be growth. Our language seemingly agrees, as it refers to adults as *grown-ups* rather than "raised people" or "tall people."

A quote attributed to author Gail Sheehy warns, "If we don't change, we don't grow." Things can be raised without changing. You could raise this book over your head to a higher plane, but it does not change the book. The pages remain the same, the words on the pages are the same, and the shape and size of the book do not change. In other words, the book does not grow by being raised over your head. Similarly, to grow Catholic children, change is necessary.

Looking at the growth of a flower, it is clear to see how a small seed changes. A flower's seed sprouts into a bud and acquires leaves as it gets physically taller until it finally blossoms into a beautiful flower. The transition—or conversion—from seed to flower is quite significant. Although not a very eloquent or scientific representation, the image of a flower changing as it gets taller parallels the idea that children's faith should change as they get physically taller. Furthermore, a flower grows in rich soil as a result of nurturing *light* and *water* (again, very simplistic and nonscientific). For children, the *light* of the world (Jesus) and the *waters* of baptism provide them the tools they need to grow. Parents have a responsibility to introduce children to these tools and see to it they are used to help them grow spiritually. If a flower is not watered, it will eventually die. If you do not nourish your faith, it also can die and it certainly will not grow.

Parents are called to plant the seeds of faith by helping children continually grow and experience the love of God and the fruits of a relationship with Jesus. When they do this, parents truly give children the opportunity not only to enjoy the Kingdom of Heaven, but also to experience the kingdom in their lives on earth. What parent would not want that for his or her child(ren)?

Jesus says it best when speaking to a crowd through the parable of the sower:

> And as [the sower] sowed, some seed fell on the path, and birds came and ate it up. Some fell on rocky ground, where it had little soil; it sprang up at once because the soil was not deep, and when the sun rose it was scorched, and it withered for lack of roots. Some seed fell among thorns, some seed fell on rich soil, and produced fruit, a hundred or sixty or thirty fold. (Matt. 13:4–8)

In Jesus's explanation of this parable in Matthew 13:19–23, He says,

> The seed sown on the path is the one who hears the word of the kingdom without understanding it, and the evil one comes and steals away what was sown in his heart. The seed sown on rocky ground is the one who hears the word and receives it at once with joy. But he has no root and lasts only for a time. When some tribulation or persecution comes because of the word, he immediately falls away. The seed sown among thorns is the one who hears the word, but then worldly anxiety and the lure of riches choke the word and it bears no fruit. But the seed sown on rich soil is the one who hears the word and understands it, who indeed bears fruit and yields a hundred or sixty or thirtyfold.

In this parable, Jesus himself is clearly asking the crowds to *grow* and bear "fruit." He is also asking all of *us* to do the same. The call for parents is to hear, understand, teach, and nourish the Good News in order to prepare children for a lifetime of spiritual growth. This has become my call since deciding not to *raise* Catholic children. Although my children will become taller Catholics in this process, they will be so much more.

---

"Finally, brothers, whatever is true, whatever is honorable, whatever is just, whatever is pure, whatever is lovely, whatever is gracious, if there is any excellence and if there is anything worthy of praise, think about these things. Keep on doing what you have learned and received and heard and seen in me. Then the God of peace will be with you" (Phil. 4:8–9).

# 33
# Rembrandt Did It

The famous artist, Rembrandt, has at least three depictions of the parable of the prodigal son (Luke 15:11–32). In 1635, he sketched the *Prodigal Son at the Tavern*, where the focus is on the celebration or the party in the parable. In 1636, he painted *Return of the Prodigal Son*, which focuses on the repentant son. He intentionally does not show the father's face because he wants the focus to be on the son begging for forgiveness. Finally, in 1665, in another *Return of the Prodigal Son*, Rembrandt shows the father's face but not the son's. His focus this time is on the compassion of the father and spiritual qualities. This is the picture I have in my home.

If a picture is worth a thousand words, I believe Rembrandt is teaching a lesson about growing in faith through these three artistic works. All three pieces of art represent the same story, but each sends a different message. More than likely, the message represents what was going on in the artist's life at the time, but it also tells us something unique about the Word of God. In my life, I am certain I have played all three roles. I have been the obedient son, the son who squandered the father's inheritance, and the forgiving father.

They call the Bible a living book because it has the ability to mean different things to each of us at different times in our lives. I am amazed at how many times I can read scripture and discover something new, especially when I listen with an open heart, even to the familiar stories. I am even more amazed by the times I share scripture stories with others, and they open up another meaning for me because of what God says to them in the story.

My husband and I have a saying about the adventures and journeys we take. When we visit a new restaurant or a new city and are not satisfied, we "mark it off the list." This phrase is our way of saying, "We did it for the sake of saying we did it, but once was enough." This is not the intention of your faith journey. Don't kid yourself into thinking that if you receive the sacrament of reconciliation this year, you can mark it off the list for another year. When you read scripture, don't assume you've heard the story before, and there is not a new lesson for you to learn by listening again. When sharing these familiar stories with others, I am always amazed at how much new insight they bring to what I already thought I knew about the story.

On the journeys my husband and I have taken, we have come across some new things we want to keep on our list of things to do. These are the things we tell our friends about and the things we will revisit over and over again. The intention of our faith journey is to revisit *and share* the Bible and the sacraments over and over again. Keep this in mind, and I promise you will grow in your faith.

Look back over the pages in this book and make a plan today for your spiritual growth. If you have read this book all the way through the first time, go back and reread each section and begin creating your to-do lists for growing. My hope is to plant the seeds and inspire you to nurture your faith from here. I have no doubt you can grow in ways far surpassing the scope of this book. Keep a journal of your experiences and don't forget to share your stories. Share the ideas you found helpful in this book with those you love, or share a copy of this book. Most important, go share the light of Christ in all you do as a growing Catholic.

# 34
# Fall into the Fall Leaves

When I taught language arts, I had a lot of fun teaching the parts of speech with words like *fall* because this word (and many others) can be more than one part of speech. In the case of the title on this page, the word *fall* is both a verb (an action) and an adjective (a word that describes something). So if you "fall in the fall leaves," the first "fall" in the sentence is the act of falling (the verb); the second is describing the leaves (the adjective). For those keeping track, the word *fall* can also be a noun (person, place, thing, or idea) that names one of the four seasons in our year.

Without boring you with a language arts lesson, I want you to be aware a similar situation exists with the title of this book. The phrase "growing Catholics" can be something you do—the act of growing Catholic children (verb) or it can be an adjective that describes the type of Catholic you are. My hope is that there are things in this book that will help you to *grow* Catholic children and things that will allow you to grow yourself so you may describe yourself as one who is growing (a growing Catholic).

In my experience, these happen concurrently, like a hug. A hug is a gift you cannot give without getting back. I find it very difficult to help others grow as a Catholic without growing a bit myself. Begin your own story of growth, and be prepared to reap the benefits of a life with Christ. Begin knowing you can travel at your own pace, and you are not alone. You have the church, Pope, bishops, priests, deacons, sisters, and all the people of God working with you in this common goal of spreading the Good News of Christ—not to mention, you also have God on your side.

Parents often leave an inheritance to their children. Sometimes this inheritance comes in the form of money, real estate, businesses, or other material assets. Oftentimes, children inherit things they do not know how to handle. For example, a large sum of money may be very foreign to children, and inheriting it may cause them to squander it away foolishly. A parent may be an adept business owner, but running the parents' business may not be the expertise of the child, making the inheritance less valuable.

I mentioned in the beginning of this book that I had inherited my parents' faith and did not have ownership in it myself. In essence, I left home with a "business" I knew nothing about how to run. Basically, I had no expertise in the faith I inherited. There is no doubt the *best* inheritance you can leave your children is faith, but you must show them how to "run the business" so they can get the most value out of it. Show them how to pray and how to read scripture. Show them the meaning of the sacraments. Help them understand the Mass. Teach them to respect the church, and prepare them for a lifelong relationship with Christ. In doing so, you will be leaving the same inheritance Christ left the apostles.

Money will go, businesses will close, material possessions will depreciate, but faith is an inheritance that will keep on living for generations. Faith is the inheritance we all have the means to leave behind, so prepare your children for it. Otherwise, don't be surprised if they squander it away and there is nothing to share with the next generation.

Although sharing or "witnessing" to your own family is the best place to start, I learned in my study that we are all truly called to do more. Jesus told his first followers to become "fishers of men" (Matt. 5:19). It was the mission given to His first followers, and that same mission is given to each of us today. By virtue of our baptism, we share in the priesthood of Christ, in his prophetic and royal mission.

# 35
# A Triple Dog Dare

As I end the pages of this book, I am reminded of a book by William H. Danforth I received as a high-school senior called, *I Dare You.* The book challenges the reader to be a leader by doing certain things. A leader is one who acts, and if a dare motivates you to act, then I would like to take advantage of the title of that book. However, since high school, I have seen the movie *A Christmas Story* and learned the phrase, "I triple dog dare you." According to the movie's narrator, a triple dog dare is a dare that cannot be ignored. There is something about a dare that motivates the human spirit to action. That is my challenge to you who are reading this book. *I triple dog dare you* to begin growing Catholics (the verb) and become a growing Catholic (the adjective) in the process.

I also invite you to share your stories of growth with me at www.growingcatholics.com. If I have learned anything from writing this book it is this: Whenever *anyone* shares a story of growth, *everyone* who shares in the story grows. We have an obligation to share.

As I send this book off, I have lit a candle in my church for all who will read it. My prayer for you is that you grow to share in the peace and love of our risen Lord and that you have the courage to share it with your children so they may share your joy.

Now go in peace to love and serve the Lord.

"You are the light of the world. A city set on a mountain cannot be hidden. Nor do they light a lamp and then put it under a bushel basket; it is set on a lampstand, where it gives light to all in the house. Just so, your light must shine before others, that they may see your good deeds and glorify your heavenly Father" (Matt. 5:14).